SERVANTS TOGETHER

Salvationist Perspectives
on Ministry

SERVANTS TOGETHER

Salvationist Perspectives on Ministry

'But you are a chosen people, a royal priesthood,
a holy nation, a people belonging to God, that you
may declare the praises of him who called you out of
darkness into his wonderful light. Once you were
not a people, but now you are the people of God;
once you had not received mercy, but now you
have received mercy'
(1 Peter 2:9, 10 *New International Version*).

Salvation Books
The Salvation Army International Headquarters
London, United Kingdom

Copyright © 2002 The General of The Salvation Army
First published 2002

Revised edition 2008

ISBN 978 0 85412 785 6

Scripture quotations, unless otherwise noted, are from the
New International Version
Copyright © 1986 by the International Bible Society

Cover art by Mickhail Gavrilov
Book design by Nathan Sigauke

Published by Salvation Books
The Salvation Army International Headquarters
101 Queen Victoria Street, London EC4V 4EH, United Kingdom

Printed by UK Territory Print & Design Unit

Contents

Page

Foreword by General Shaw Clifton — xi
Foreword to the 2002 edition by General John Gowans — xiii
Explanatory note — xv
Introduction — xvii

SECTION ONE
THE CALLING OF GOD'S PEOPLE
Introduction — 1

Chapter One
WORSHIP — 3
    To love God — 4
    Sharpening our sight — 4
    Hearing God in sounds — 5
    Hearing God in the silence — 6
    Bringing everything into God's presence through prayer — 6
    Worship expressed in discipleship — 7
    Today and tomorrow — 8
        For group discussion — 9

Chapter Two
COMMUNITY — 11
    Incarnational community — 12
    Unity in diversity — 14

The community as the Body of Christ	15
A community of friends	16
A community of saints	17
Soldiers at war	18
A community of hope	20
For group discussion	20

Chapter Three
MISSION	21
A living icon of Christ	22
The Great Commission	23
Mission as practical deeds	25
Mission as preaching	26
Mission as dialogue	27
Mission as crossing boundaries: the mission principle of Paul	28
Mission of hope	30
For group discussion	30

SECTION TWO
THE MINISTRY OF GOD'S PEOPLE
Introduction	33

Chapter Four
VOCATION	35
Vocation in the New Testament	35
Vocation in the Church	36
Vocation in today's Church	39
For group discussion	40

Chapter Five
PRIESTHOOD	41
Priesthood in the Old Testament	41
Priesthood in the New Testament	42

Priesthood in the Church	44
Priesthood in today's Church	46
For group discussion	48

Chapter Six

SPIRITUAL GIFTING AND SPIRITUAL FRUITS	49
Old Testament understanding	52
New Testament teaching	52
Unity and diversity	55
Gifts of leadership	57
Quenching the Spirit	58
Gifting in today's Church	59
The Fruits of the Holy Spirit	61
For group discussion	62

SECTION THREE
THE LEADERSHIP OF GOD'S PEOPLE – ITS SCOPE

Introduction	63

Chapter Seven

COMMISSIONING	67
Commissioning in the New Testament	68
An example from Church history	69
Commissioning in The Salvation Army	70
For group discussion	73

Chapter Eight

ORDAINED TO SERVANT LEADERSHIP	75
Ordination in The Salvation Army	76
Ordination from a biblical perspective	83
Ordination and commissioning of officers in The Salvation Army	84
The uniqueness of Salvation Army officership	86

Spiritual and servant leadership	89
For group discussion	92
Chief of the Staff's Minute on Commissioning	93

Chapter Nine
CONSULTATIVE MINISTRY	107
A Trinitarian pattern	109
The Body of Christ	110
Mutual recognition of gifts	112
A challenging opportunity	114
For group discussion	115

SECTION FOUR
THE LEADERSHIP OF GOD'S PEOPLE – ITS CHARACTER
Introduction	117

Chapter Ten
PRIESTLY AND PROPHETIC ROLES	119
The Old Testament	120
New Testament teaching	121
In the history of the Church	122
In The Salvation Army	124
For group discussion	125

Chapter Eleven
TRUE LEADERSHIP	127
1. Calling	128
2. Spiritual depth	129
3. Courage	130
4. Personal discipline	132
5. Relationship-building	133
6. Servanthood	134
7. Empowerment of others	135

8. Creativity	136
9. Passion for mission	137
10. Personal and vocational growth	138
For group discussion	140

Chapter Twelve
THE FUTURE OF LEADERSHIP 143
1. Calling in a world driven by competition 144
2. Spiritual depth in a world of shallowness 146
3. Courage in a world of fear-driven caution 148
4. Personal discipline in a world without focus 149
5. Relationship-building in an alienated world 150
6. Servanthood in a world of self-centredness 151
7. Empowerment of others in a power-grasping world 152
8. Creativity in a world of conformity 153
9. Passion for mission in a rootless world 154
10. Personal and vocational growth in a changing and complex world 155
Who is sufficient? 157
For group discussion *157*

CONCLUSION 159
THE DISCIPLINES 161

Foreword

IT affords me great pleasure to introduce and recommend this revised and updated edition of *Servants Together – Salvationist Perspectives on Ministry*.

General Gowans' Foreword to the original 2002 edition (see next page) still speaks powerfully to us all and therefore I do not need to spell out in detail what the book is about.

I am more than content to encourage warmly all Salvationists to read it and to make much use of it for group discussion, hoping that the Army's mission-effectiveness and our devotion to Christ will be thereby deepened.

May God bless this new edition to his lasting glory.

Shaw Clifton
General

London, July 2008

Foreword to the 2002 edition

SALVATIONISTS pride themselves on being 'doers of the word and not hearers only', and the emphasis we place on rolling up our sleeves and getting on with it is one with which I heartily agree. But action without reflection soon becomes mindless routine; we must continually review what we are doing and why we do it. There is, of course, an even more fundamental need: to examine in the light of Scripture who we are as a people, and where The Salvation Army fits into the historic Church – that mysterious 'Body of Christ' which God uses, in his mystical mercy, to continue the work of his Son in the world.

This need was recognised by Salvation Army leaders meeting in conference in Hong Kong in 1995, when they recommended, 'That the roles of officers and soldiers be defined and a theology of lay (non-officer) priesthood be developed to encourage greater involvement in ministry'. General Paul Rader, my distinguished predecessor, asked the International Doctrine Council to address this recommendation, which they have done with thoroughness, wisdom and care to produce the volume now in your hands.

This book is not, of course, Holy Writ. It represents rather a helpful bringing out and gathering together of the theology that many Salvationists would agree underlies and informs the particular view we have of ourselves and our work. It is my great hope that all who take up *Servants Together* will be enlightened and stimulated as they read, but even more that they will indeed be led to greater involvement in ministry.

John Gowans
General
London, 2002

Explanatory note regarding *Salvation Story*

A NUMBER of references are made in this book to *Salvation Story*, first published in 1998 as a successor publication to The Salvation Army's 1969 edition of the *Handbook of Doctrine*.

Previous publications outlining the Army's doctrinal stance included *Rules and Doctrines of the Christine Mission*, published in 1875; *The Doctrines and Disciplines of The Salvation Army*, prepared in 1881 and published two years later; and *The Doctrines of The Salvation Army*, published in 1885. Various editions of this were subsequently produced. In 1922 a new *Handbook of Salvation Army Doctrine* was published, and new editions were published in 1925, 1927 and 1935. From the 1927 edition onwards, the title was changed to *The Salvation Army Handbook of Doctrine*. A new *Handbook of Doctrine* was published in 1969. This was reprinted several times, but was not revised until work started on *Salvation Story*.

The early doctrinal handbooks were expositions of the principal doctrines of The Salvation Army as set out in its Deed Poll of 1878. These reveal how the faith of Salvationists is grounded in Scripture, and *Salvation Story* was written – in the words of General Paul Rader's foreword to that book – 'to assist us in reflecting on the foundation of that faith, and its meaning for our life together as the people of God in mission and for our programmes of redemptive and compassionate action'.

Salvation Story was written after General Eva Burrows mandated the International Doctrine Council in 1992 to prepare a new *Handbook of Doctrine* with a fresh approach. *Salvation Story* – still very much in use today throughout the Army world – was the fulfilment of that charge.

Introduction

BY God's grace, all believers are in ministry: we are *Servants Together*. Such ministry has both biblical and theological foundations, and it is important to understand and appropriate those foundations in order to establish a vision for ministry that will be useful for The Salvation Army. Our ministry is grounded in our understanding of ourselves as the people of God. We are servants of Christ who are called to worship him, to be together in community and to be sent out into the world in mission.

Salvation Army theology has sometimes tended towards a theology of the individual rather than of the Church. Section One of this book is careful to place the concept of ministry in the broader theological context of the calling of all of God's people to a discipleship of worship, community and mission. The Church is seen as a worshipping community intent on corporate as well as individual mission, with worship and community being integral to a biblical understanding of ministry.

The sub-heading of the book – 'The Ministry of the Whole People of God' – finds its development in Section Two. Three primary theological foundations are here identified as being indispensable to the ministry of God's people: a theology of vocation, a theology of the biblical concept of priesthood, and a theology of the gifts and fruits of the Holy Spirit.

Section Three marks a change in focus as it introduces the subject of the leadership of God's people. That subject cannot of course be divorced from the concept of the priesthood of all believers. Leaders in the Christian Church are themselves part of the priesthood of all believers, part of the people of God. To employ a term frequently used in many denominations of the Church – they too are 'laity'. In The Salvation Army, officers and others in leadership positions are first of all soldiers. They exercise their leadership gift as one among the many gifts of the 'laos' – the New Testament Greek term for the whole 'people of God'.

This section, on the scope of leadership, begins by recognising that many within the Body of Christ and The Salvation Army in particular are 'commissioned' to ministries of servant leadership. It concludes on a similar note by seeing leadership as a 'servants together' team. But among those so commissioned as members of that team there is a heritage of the commissioning of Salvation Army officers that in 1978 was identified with the term ordination. Chapter Eight traces the history of that change as it emphasises that ordination in the Army is not to be regarded as an ordination to status but an ordination to servanthood.

The final section of the book deals with the character of the leadership of God's people – its priestly and prophetic roles, an understanding of what is involved in true leadership and a visionary picture concerning the future of leadership in the Army. Jesus Christ is the ultimate model of such leadership ideals. His ministry similarly is the guide for the ministry of the whole people of God. Servants together today are therefore called to have the same attitude as that of Jesus Christ, who 'made himself nothing, taking the very nature of a servant' (Philippians 2:7). Inasmuch as we take on that likeness, we are the Body of Christ, reflecting the face of Jesus Christ in the world today, as the cover of this book, designed by Salvationist Mickhail Gavrilov from Russia, illustrates.

SECTION ONE

THE CALLING OF GOD'S PEOPLE

Introduction

WORDS carry an amazing power. They can reveal, redeem, rebuild, and heal, isolate, conceal, hurt and destroy. There is wonder in words because we can communicate and express ourselves through them and the world opens up for us. When God calls us he calls in words through our many different languages. Throughout history God has also spoken and called in other kinds of languages which we can understand. He has spoken through the languages of beauty and creativity, of joy and fullness of life, of love and fulfilment, of fellowship and communion, of stillness and solitude, of loneliness and emptiness, of suffering and isolation. Through all these languages the reality of God is revealed to us and has been written down and contained within both the richness and limitation of words in the Bible.

Most profoundly God has spoken through his Son Jesus Christ. Jesus used different languages to show what God was like. Among these the languages of healing and compassion were profound. Through them he called people into fellowship with God. He not only spoke the words of God, he himself is the Word of God, who brings salvation to the world and saves today as in days past.

In the ministry of Jesus there were two words especially which were life changing for individual persons. We hear the same two words from the risen Christ. They have altered the course of history wherever and whenever they have been spoken and received. The words are: 'Follow me!'

This is the call to discipleship. These words cause us to break out of our previous life and to break through into a totally new life. This new life is the Kingdom of God. It is a life in service to the Kingdom of God in this present world. This causes a new orientation in life, an orientation according to Kingdom values. It results in a life of discipleship, sustained by his gifts of grace and the continuing call of Christ.

The call to discipleship is not to a limited time of apprenticeship, but to a lifelong commitment to follow in the footsteps of Christ. It is a call to live a life of holiness through our different vocations.

It is a call to holiness expressed in these three essentials:

Worship

Community

Mission

Chapter Two

WORSHIP

WE are called to worship. Worship is an encounter with God where we meet him through a variety of languages and through all our senses. Our whole life is an act of worship, a continuing encounter with God where we turn our attention to him to the extent that each of us can say: 'I am a prayer.'

In Romans 12:1, 2 Paul urges us to enter into an act of worship in view of the mercy of God. This worship encompasses both body and mind and is truly holistic. We surrender our body with all its senses, with all its life – this is an unconditional gift, a holy gift pleasing to God. Instead of conforming to the spirit of the time we are being transformed by a renewal of our minds to rethink and repent. Through this act of worship and renewal we can judge what the will of God is.

This is a strong description of our whole life lived as an act of worship. It rejects the division of life into different compartments – one for work, one for pleasure, one for family and friends, one for religious activities and so on. Such compartmentalisation disconnects us. It reduces worship to an entity of its own instead of allowing it to be a natural part of our whole life.

The text in Romans encourages us to surrender our daily life (symbolised by our body) as a gift and to let our minds or our common sense be renewed and transformed. When we do this we experience the all-encompassing renewal which alters our thinking and makes us powerful tools in the hands of God.

To love God

Worship is in essence an act of love, an expression of love. The greatest commandment is: 'Love the Lord your God with all your heart and with all your soul and with all your mind and with all your strength' (Mark 12:30).

This commandment shows the intensity and depth of the love to which God calls us. It is a love which involves our total being by our full strength. God calls forth our strength because he knows it is there and he wants to activate it into a full life of love.

To express this love we do not constantly try to feel love or assess our capacity for love. We simply get on with living. By the grace of God we have been given this life to live. The sheer joy of life and love of life can be worship. It can be a form of praise to God, the creator of all. He wants us to love to live.

Sharpening our sight

Viewing our whole life and being as an act of worship is the cornerstone of our life with God. Around that vision we need to create visible and concrete acts of worship, places where we meet and share fellowship, places where we have our sight sharpened because we consciously seek the presence of God.

'Seeing' is a powerful act of worship which we have often underestimated. To see a candle burning, to let the eye rest on beautiful flowers or pieces of art can facilitate worship and close encounters with God. When we join each other in worship, the arrangement of the room is vital. If it is ugly or not well prepared we have to set this important sense of seeing aside, we have to close our eyes or try to focus on other senses and miss the visual dimension of worship. Our buildings, furniture, colours and material can all support our worship through seeing.

The visual parts of worship are important in action as well. Dance, drama, movements, kneeling – all these visual expressions strengthen our worship.

Corporate worship presents many opportunities for sharpening our sight. This worship in community requires openness towards God and each other, a willingness to share, to be vulnerable and to be challenged. It requires a love for the people of God and for the fellowship he has given, a love for the lost world and an urgent desire to be in the presence of God as part of his people. With such an attitude we enter into a genuine fellowship and here we have our eyes opened so that we can see.

Hearing God in sounds

We worship through the words of the Scriptures, of the sermon, of the prayers, of the songs and of the testimonies. We are blessed when these means of grace bear the marks of a genuine encounter with God and when they are perfected to his glory through his presence.

There is a significance to the spoken word which we must never forget. To read the Scriptures, reflect upon them and relate the message to our situation is crucial for our worship. We need this for spiritual growth and nourishment. It has been a vital element of Christian worship through the centuries. It has its roots in synagogue tradition, as is reflected in the way Jesus expounded the Scriptures in Nazareth (see Luke 4:16-21). The apostles preached the word and their letters were read by the young churches for teaching and nourishment. To Titus Paul writes: 'He must hold firmly to the trustworthy message as it has been taught, so that he can encourage others by sound doctrine and refute those who oppose it' (Titus 1:9). We believe that, as the Scriptures are inspired by God, so we will be assisted by the Holy Spirit when listening to and proclaiming the message.

Music has become one of our most cherished tools of worship. It unites us. Many of our songs reflect worship as a corporate act. God's greatness deserves countless multitudes singing to his glory: 'O for a thousand tongues to sing my great redeemer's praise'

(Charles Wesley). When we join in the singing we worship with our whole being and when we listen to the music we 'hear' the testimonies from past and present, we hear the voice of God calling us.

Hearing God in the silence

We Salvationists are not as well trained in hearing God in the silence as in hearing him in the sounds. With many other people of today, we are also rediscovering the wonder of worship in silence.

The Orthodox Church calls itself the church of silence. Silence is seen as an expression of awe because God can come in the silence (1 Kings 19:11, 12) more than in the mighty manifestations. The Quaker tradition is built on silence in worship. The silence is a condition for listening to God. The essence of prayer is not so much our words, but an offering of ourselves and a willingness to listen.

We need times of silence when we step back, reflect and refrain from filling up time with our activities and words. This is a vital act of worship. It is a fountain of new life and strength. Silence can be frightening unless we discipline ourselves for it and learn to live with it. In the silence our whole being turns into prayer because we are in the presence of God in our nakedness of spirit, our poverty, our sins and our broken words. Here we are given rest, healing and peace. For Jesus said, 'Come to me, all you who are weary and burdened, and I will give you rest' (Matthew 11:28).

Bringing everything into the presence of God through prayer

We have a strong tradition of personal, spontaneous prayers in our worship, often to the exclusion of written, liturgical prayers. This tradition is of great value and should be nourished in the teaching of our people from early childhood or early Christian life, as it is a spring of power and new life. Even though that priority should be kept, written and liturgical prayers can have an immense impact in worship and be a means of blessing as well as a teaching tool in the quest for a dynamic prayer life. We can draw upon prayers from church history as well as write them ourselves.

In a novel by the Swedish writer Sven Delblanc, *The Daughters of Samuel*, the poor widow Cecilie gets a pair of glasses from her children for her birthday present. They are very much needed. These glasses become both a joy and a pain to her. Her sight improves and her work gets easier, but now she is also able to see the bitterness and poverty in the faces of her children. She notices the hopelessness. She turns this experience into a prayer: 'Don't make the world so cruel that I want blindness as a gift! That is all I dare to pray, Thou good and merciful God!' Her prayer is like the old biblical prayers which contain cries for help and for a more just world. She doesn't ask for liberation from the sharp sight that notices both joy and pain. She asks that she will never reach the point where the pain and cruelty become her whole horizon.

Our prayer life could be illustrated by such a pair of glasses. Through prayer we get a sharp and clear sight of our own reality and the reality of the world around us. We bring everything into God's presence when we praise him for all he is and all he does. We bring to him our pain and the sharpness of our protest as we pray, 'Deliver us from evil.' We come with our petitions, the most natural part of prayer, and with our intercessions, our open acts of love for others.

Prayer sharpens our sight and our hearing and fills our silence with God's rest and peace.

Worship expressed in discipleship

The biblical words for worship are, at their roots, words for service. This implies a deep connection between Christian worship and service. They are essentially one.

The most common Hebrew words for worship have 'ebed', which means servant, as their root. This root word describes all sorts of service. In the New Testament the two words used for worship are 'latreia', which means service and worship (see Romans 12:1), and 'leitourgia', which was used in everyday language as service to the community or state, usually without pay (see Hebrews 10:11).

Our life as an act of worship directs us towards true discipleship.

In Isaiah 58:6-7 we are given directions for this life: 'Is not this the kind of fasting I have chosen: to loose the chains of injustice and untie the cords of the yoke, to set the oppressed free and break every yoke? Is it not to share your food with the hungry and to provide the poor wanderer with shelter – when you see the naked, to clothe him, and not to turn away from your own flesh and blood?' Jesus told the story of the good Samaritan to illustrate that love for God demands unconditional love for our neighbours (Luke 10:25-37).

The true disciple does not separate worship from compassionate service, nor fail to see the holy in the everyday.

Today and tomorrow

Salvationists sometimes sing the chorus, 'This is the day that the Lord has made', and by this we point to the fact that, when we worship, the present tense is all-important. We are meeting God now – today. The Holy Spirit is contemporary and present today. But to the 'today' of our worship belong tomorrow and yesterday. The salvation story's 'then' is the foundation for our celebration today, and at the centre of the message is the Christian hope that 'one day ...'.

In worship we are reminded of the message that a fallen world is being recreated, that it is moving towards becoming a new Heaven and a new earth (Revelation 21:1). When we live our lives as an act of worship, we are able to enter the flow of this new creation. There is a word which breathes through this life of recreated discipleship. It is the word of faith, hope and love: 'Maranatha – Lord come!' The people of God are called to worship. There they meet God and reshape their lives for the present and future of his coming. There they give themselves to service, which is their worship in the world. There they come to know themselves as the community of God.

* * *

For group discussion

1. Discuss the different languages God uses when he calls us. Give examples from personal experience.

2. Discuss how to make worship meaningful for you as a fellowship, as well as to you as an individual.

3. Which components of worship do you think are needed to feed the spiritual hunger of people of today?

Chapter Two

COMMUNITY

WE are called into community. The Christian community is not just any fellowship. It is a specific sort of fellowship, a communion with Christ.

The New Testament uses the word 'koinonia', a fellowship that comes into being when we have a share in something, when we are involved in or initiated into something, not when we simply gather around something.

This something shared is actually someone, Jesus Christ. 'Koinonia' comes into being when we are initiated into Christ. We die to ourselves and are raised into Christ (Romans 6:4). When we live in Christ, we live a life that feeds upon Christ, a life that draws its nutriment and vitality from Christ.

We can test a fellowship to see if it is a genuine 'koinonia' or not by asking this question: Is it a fellowship defined by its religious activities or is it a communion with Christ?

A religious fellowship centred on Christ can be a fellowship of ideology rather than the biblical one, which is life-giving and life-sustaining. To avoid barrenness and to nurture a life of discipleship, our communion must be intimate and personal with Christ and marked by openness to each other.

It must reflect the true communion written on the heart of the Triune God.

> *God created humanity because love expressed in community is the very essence of his nature, not because of any incompleteness within himself. As human beings,*

we are created in the image of God with a nature to relate to one another. We reach our fulfilment only in community with him and with one another. Without him and without each other, we lack wholeness and the possibility of maturing through developing relationships. God, then, is always in fellowship within himself and with us (Salvation Story, Chapter 2, 'A God in fellowship').

We are called into this communion. The first letter to John describes this calling: 'That which was from the beginning, which we have heard, which we have seen with our eyes, which we have looked at and our hands have touched ... We proclaim to you what we have seen and heard, so that you also may have fellowship with us. And our fellowship is with the Father and with his Son, Jesus Christ' (1 John 1:1, 3).

This communion is an event of grace as our lives are touched in the very depths of our being and transformed into Christlikeness. The fellowship is built on a sure foundation, the living Word. But it is not a static fellowship. While its calling remains the same, it develops and adjusts itself as circumstances change and as it is touched by the world and by people.

Incarnational community

Even though the fellowship belongs to the Kingdom of God, it is lived out in this world. Fellowships consist of people who belong together, who understand each other either by speaking the same language or understanding each other's language.

God revealed himself in Jesus Christ at a specific time in history, at a specific place and within a specific people. Our fellowships are also lived at a certain time in history, in this third millennium, that brings its own challenges to us. Rapid development, social unrest, mobility of people, disparity among people and new technology mark this time. The biblical idea of community seems alien for the majority, who at the same time are longing for genuine fellowship. It is a time when more and more are escaping into false fellowships. In this historical moment, it is especially important that the signs of a biblical community identify our fellowship. People will then be able to recognise those who are in close communion with God, a community that reaches out to them and welcomes them in.

Our fellowships are expressions of the places we live in and the culture connected to these places. The cultures of countries and continents differ and within countries there are varieties of cultures, the main cultures and then subcultures of all kinds. There are city cultures, rural cultures, youth cultures, children's cultures, women's cultures, immigrant cultures, the cultures of the elite, the cultures of the oppressed and so on. The different fellowships must reflect these to be truly incarnational.

A true Christian community is incarnational. As God brought salvation to the human race by becoming incarnate ('enfleshed') in Jesus of Nazareth, a member of first-century Palestinian Jewish culture, so his community, the Church, continues his saving mission by entering specific cultures and taking on the 'flesh' of those cultures. Nineteenth-century British Salvationists effectively reached tens of thousands of working class people because they adopted the language, styles and concerns of that culture and paid the price of this incarnational movement.

The Christian community reflects different cultures and people. At the same time, it transcends all cultures and is also countercultural, because it feeds on the eternal Christ.

We have a unique Salvationist culture, which is both international and national, crossing and breaking down boundaries which otherwise separate people. It expresses itself as an incarnational fellowship by reflecting all sorts of cultures and people in a unity consisting of considerable diversity. But most importantly it is an incarnational community because it stresses the unique value of the life given to us as a gift of God. The focal point is that God valued human life so much that he sent his Son into this world as a human being to relieve human suffering and to save us. One of the fundamental purposes of this fellowship is to continue the mission of Christ in relieving human suffering and pointing to his salvation. This incarnational community is a token of the true Christian fellowship, fulfilled when Christ becomes all in all.

Unity in diversity

True fellowship finds unity in diversity. The unity of Christ's community is not uniformity. There is not only room for variety, there is the necessity for it. A variety of gifts and abilities will come to the surface and be expressed as the fellowship meets various concrete challenges.

The unity of the fellowship is also expressed in solidarity. Spiritual as well as material needs are met by a sharing of resources. The ideal of this solidarity among the early Christians is recorded in the early chapters of Acts. Such solidarity has been repeated again and again throughout Church history, especially in times of oppression when unity had to be expressed very concretely for the Christian community to survive.

We need a growing understanding of this aspect of Christian unity today. We need mutual sharing of resources spiritually, educationally and economically among different cultures and countries. Often we focus on material needs and that is important, but we must not forget the solidarity in sharing and appreciating spiritual wealth.

Even though Christ's fellowship is lived out within a certain culture it is not bound to that culture or place. It is a universal fellowship because it feeds upon Christ, the Saviour of the world, who calls into fellowship people of all races, genders and ages – 'There is neither Jew nor Greek, slave nor free, male nor female, for you are all one in Christ Jesus' (Galatians 3:28).

Acknowledgment of its universal nature is the Christian fellowship's protection against one-sided nationalism and the identification of Christianity with a certain culture. The Church always looks beyond itself to new borders to cross and cultures to enter. It embraces the rich diversity. It expresses discipleship in a kaleidoscope of cultural patterns. The very diversity of the Church is the most powerful witness to the Church's universality.

At Pentecost the Holy Spirit gave the gift of speaking many languages as a sign of the universal nature of the Christian fellowship.

In the story of the tower of Babel many languages caused confusion, division and destroyed fellowship. In the story of Pentecost the same manifestation brought salvation, unity, fellowship and recognition, because God the Holy Spirit is the Spirit of unity and universality.

The Church is one jewel with myriad facets.

The community as the Body of Christ

The Christian community is described in a number of ways in the New Testament. Here are just four examples: the Body of Christ, the friends of Christ, a community of saints and soldiers at war.
Paul uses the image of the body to explain this unique fellowship. It is an organic image with all the possibilities for parts of that body to experience growth and decay. By using this image of life all aspects of the living body can be taken into consideration to give as broad an application as possible. This image illustrates that:

- Churches can grow and develop strength and power.
- Churches can repair themselves when wounded or assaulted by illness and accidents.
- Churches can adapt to changing needs.
- Churches can bear and give birth to new life.
- Churches can constantly renew themselves.

But also that, within our churches:

- There is vulnerability and frailty.
- There is the possibility of under-development.
- There is the possibility of dehydration and malnutrition.
- There is the possibility of decay and death.
- There is the hope of resurrection.

In our Salvationist fellowship we are sometimes confronted with parts of the Body that are suffering, weak and sick; and our calling includes incorporating weak parts into our church body. We work with many weak and even dysfunctional people. We strongly believe that the community can heal and restore itself and transform weakness into strength, because we are the Body of a healing Christ.

If the fellowship is founded in Christ, and is truly the Body of Christ, then its core is sound with the potential for growth, strength and adaptation. In this community of Christ, the Holy Spirit keeps reviving and energising the Body.

A community of friends

In the Gospel of John, Jesus used the word 'friend' to define the relationship between his disciples and himself. 'Greater love has no one than this, that he lay down his life for his friends. You are my friends if you do what I command. I no longer call you servants, because a servant does not know his master's business. Instead, I have called you friends, for everything that I learned from my Father I have made known to you' (John 15:13-15).

Friendship is a free relationship which we have chosen. It is built on recognition of a humanity we treasure, of shared values and, very often, of shared circumstances and interests. We are not forced into friendships by geographical, social, biological or economic necessity, as can be the case with many of our other relationships.

Friendship is an open relationship that can be extended to include many more. Part of the nature of true friendship is that it opens up to include the friend's other friends.

The core of friendship is sharing. Jesus is underlining this point when he speaks of sharing with his friends and taking them into his confidence. He even uses the word 'everything': he shares with us, his friends, everything he had learned from his Father.

In Antoine de Saint-Exupéry's novel *The Little Prince* the main theme is friendship. The little prince has a rose as his friend and he takes good care of that rose. He takes its well-being as his responsibility. One of the sentences which explains why this rose has a unique value is: 'It is the time you have spent on your rose which makes it so important.' This story has an important word to say about the life of our Salvation Army corps. It is the time and energy we invest in the fellowship which makes it so important. Jesus not only invested time and energy, but also laid down his life (John 15:13). Out of that ultimate investment in friendship a unique fellowship was born, a fellowship of Jesus' friends.

A community of saints

Sainthood is corporate as well as personal. In his letters Paul constantly describes the Christians as saints, so there are saints in Corinth, throughout Achaia, in Ephesus, in Philippi and at Colosse. In Romans 1:7 he speaks of those 'who are loved by God and called to be saints'. He uses this description 45 times. This shows that we are saints in fellowship as well as in a personal relationship with God. It is in the Christian community, which is Christ's Body, that we are nurtured and taught and where we experience Christ's sanctifying presence as a fellowship. From this community we are sent out to be the people of God in the world.

We are not saints because we are morally perfect, neither are our Christian communities perfect. We are saints because we are chosen by God and indwelt by Christ. Paul's first letter to the Corinthian church is addressed 'to those sanctified in Christ Jesus and called to be holy'.

The saints in Corinth misunderstood how the holy life should be lived. Nevertheless they are still called saints.

As those who are loved by God, we are set aside from this world and united with him. It is God's love, his call and his choice of us, his filling and forming that make us holy (Acts 4:31; Galatians 4:19). Our holiness, our status as saints, is a costly one, because it came about by the life, ministry, suffering, death and resurrection of Jesus Christ. We must keep this in mind as we are constantly challenged by the call to consecrate ourselves to him and to live in a fellowship of consecration. Some Christians, for different reasons, are separated from a regular Christian fellowship. The community of saints is a spiritual reality because we are incorporated into the Body of Christ. Whether we experience the fellowship regularly or rarely, our joy is that we are one with each other and may reach one another in Christ through the ministry of faith and prayer and so receive Christ's sanctifying grace.

Soldiers at war

As we belong to The Salvation Army, the image of the Christian community as a community of soldiers is close to our understanding and experience. Paul urges Timothy (2 Timothy 2:3, 4) to be a good soldier of Christ Jesus, and in Ephesians 6:10-17 writes about the armour of God.

This community is unique in its focus. It has a clear task. It involves proper training, total trust in one another and obedience to our commander, Jesus Christ. He plans the battle, he leads the battle and he alone must be obeyed to win the battle. In 2 Timothy 2:4 Paul writes: 'No one serving as a soldier gets involved in civilian affairs – he wants to please his commanding officer.' This community exists solely to please Christ and to follow him in battle.

Catherine Booth – Co-Founder of The Salvation Army with her husband, William Booth – expressed this truth in the following way:

> 'Soldiers of Christ must be abandoned to the war. They must be thoroughly committed to God's side; there can be no neutrals in this warfare. When the soldier enlists and takes the queen's shilling, he ceases to be his own property, becoming the property of his country, going where he is sent, standing at any post to which he is assigned, even if it be at the cannon's mouth. He gives up the ways and comforts of civilians and goes forth with his life in his hand, in obedience to the will of his sovereign. If I understand it, that is just what Jesus Christ demands of every one of his soldiers, and nothing less.'

Paul's plea in 2 Timothy is to, 'Endure hardship with us like a good soldier of Christ Jesus' (2:3). The community of soldiers is prepared to endure hardship and to share that hardship in the battle for the sake of Christ and his Kingdom. A community of soldiers is a community of commitment where we, the soldiers, are prepared to give up ourselves, our own security and health, even our own lives to fight evil and win the battle for Christ, the great Commander.

In the community of soldiers there must always be a place of healing to take the wounded and maimed, a clinic where they can rest and get proper treatment to be restored and made fit to fight again. It is an essential responsibility of soldiers to take their wounded comrades to this place, for the task of the community is salvation, as General William Booth clearly stated in 1879: 'We are a salvation people – this is our speciality – getting saved and keeping saved, and then getting somebody else saved, and then getting saved ourselves more and more' (William Booth, *The Salvationist*, January 1879).

A community of hope

This fellowship is grounded in the hope of the Resurrection. The hope reaches beyond this life when it confirms that in the destruction of death is the triumph of life. We as a fellowship will not develop our full potential until faith and love are drawn into the hope of Christ's Kingdom and we allow the future that God has in store to transform our present lives. We are reborn to a living hope.

God is our hope, but we are also his hope! He has created us to fulfil his plan for us, a plan unfolded in the Bible. The Bible is the story of God's hope. It is the story that tells us that one day there will be coherence between promise and reality, hope and experience. It is a story that invites God's people to live by that hope. The book of Revelation confirms this hope in this way: 'I am making everything new!' (21:5). This is not an expression of unrealistic optimism, but of true faith. The Christian community is marked by hope.

* * *

For group discussion

1. Identify which aspects of community you recognise in your own corps fellowship.

2. What aspects of community should your corps fellowship develop, and how can they be developed?

3. How can you individually contribute to broaden your corps fellowship so it reflects all these different aspects of community?

Chapter Three

MISSION

WE are called to mission. It is foundational to Christian discipleship to be in mission wherever we are. This is reflected very clearly in our task as Salvationists: we are 'saved to save'.

Mission conveys the biblical idea of being sent, which is so clearly expressed in John 17 and John 20. John 17 could be called a mission statement. It has to do with sending and with the content and context of that sending. The Greek word 'apostellein' – to send – is used seven times in the chapter. We first have the mission of Jesus (verses 1-5), then the mission of the disciples (6-19) and, finally, the ongoing mission (20-26). Unity and love are strong foundations for any mission. The disciples are sent 'into' the world, they live 'in' the world, but they are not 'of' the world.

Jesus says in John 20:21: 'Peace be with you! As the Father has sent me, I am sending you.' Jesus is the sender and the disciples are the ones being sent. They were fearful and doubting, but they were sent out nevertheless. Fear and doubt were overcome because they held on to what was most important. They gathered in worship on the day of the Resurrection. They placed themselves in a situation where the risen Christ could touch them. They were reached as a fellowship that had an attitude of worship on the day the power of resurrection was being manifested. They were given the Holy Spirit to continue the mission of Christ, a mission of reconciliation to this world.

Paul also describes in different ways what it means to be in mission. In 2 Corinthians 3:3 he uses the image of a letter from Christ: 'You show that you are a letter from Christ, the result of our ministry, written not with ink but with the Spirit of the living God, not on tablets of stone but on tablets of human hearts.' The basic meaning of mission as being sent is kept in that image.

In 2 Corinthians 5:20 we read: 'We are therefore Christ's ambassadors, as though God were making his appeal through us. We implore you on Christ's behalf: Be reconciled to God.' Paul calls our mission a ministry of reconciliation. The notion of being sent is again underlined in this description as well.

A living icon of Christ

Mission is a personal responsibility and privilege. It encompasses everything that Jesus sends his people into the world to be and to do; it means to be a living icon of Christ. An icon is something that reflects another reality, especially the reality of God. It doesn't claim a resemblance as that of a photo or portrait. It is seen as a window to God or, more accurately, a window from God through which he reveals himself to the world. So to be a living icon of Christ is to be such a window. Icons are used as an essential part of Eastern Orthodox worship in the churches as well as in homes, and to use this image of an icon, of being a living icon, means that our lives are Christ-centred to the extent that his marks are seen in our lives.

The very different images which Jesus used about himself with his 'I am' statements show the breadth of being an icon of Christ. Through these descriptions of his own mission, he shows us different ways in which we can be in mission. We all have different and unique gifts, but we are all called to be his witnesses.

Here are the 'I am' statements found in the Gospel of John:

> 'I am the bread of life.'
> 'I am the light of the world.'
> 'I am the door.'
> 'I am the good shepherd.'

'I am the resurrection and the life.'
'I am the way, the truth and the life.'
'I am the true vine.'

Some of the ways these can be reflected in our mission are:

- The bread of life – the gift of giving nourishment and of being nourishment to each other in the Christian community and to people who hunger to be fed in body, mind and spirit.
- The light of the world – the gift of lighting up the darkness, of giving direction, of shedding light upon matters and reflecting the light of God.
- The door – the gift of being the transition point in people's lives, of opening up the possibilities of a new life, of making a breach into closed worlds.
- The shepherd – the gift of caring and of taking responsibility.
- The resurrection and the life – the gifts of energising, vitalising and calling renewed life and commitment into being.
- The way and the truth – the gift of building foundations based on the truth of God on which people can walk through life.
- The true vine – the gift of creativity, of fruitfulness.

While we recognise the limitations of our reflection of Christ, we nevertheless embrace these means of mission. In these ways we begin to understand what it means to be a sharer in the work of Christ.

The Great Commission

In Matthew 28:19-20 we find the Great Commission, in other languages called the mission command. It has frequently been used to interpret the meaning of mission. At times the first verb 'go' has been underlined at the expense of the others. It is important as it describes the sending. Because of the focus on going, mission has at times mistakenly been understood as mission to faraway places, the further away the more the mission.

To go means that we are sent out. There is a sender who is the risen Christ, and we are sent out on the basis of his life and service, his suffering and death and resurrection. We are told to whom we are going – people of all nations. This means that we are .in mission everywhere and that we have a mission to everyone. We are never 'out of mission' once we have recognised our sending. We live our whole life in mission so that the way we react to other people, to their needs, to their attitudes and to their life determines our mission. Mission is as much an act of loving and caring as of verbal witnessing.

The Great Commission also gives us the content of the assignment: to 'make disciples'. This is a long-term process that requires a commitment from us towards the people who are the subjects of our mission. Nobody is born as a complete disciple: discipleship is taught and learned. Our task is to make disciples through example, teaching and commitment. Corps need to be places where disciples are made.

The three essentials for discipleship to which we must lead others are: witnessing, spiritual baptism and teaching. In Luke's version of this commission in Luke 24:46, 47 and Acts 1:8 the task of being a witness is given focus. The witness is to the suffering and resurrection of Christ with a message of reconciliation to all nations. This is to begin in Jerusalem and then spread further and further. The witness starts at the centre (always where we are) and then spreads out from there. The word 'witness' (in Greek 'martus') soon had the extended meaning of one suffering persecution and death because of witnessing. This is reflected in our use of the word 'martyr'. As early as Acts 22:20 there is an allusion to the witness being a martyr. We must not forget that this is a present-day reality for Christians in many parts of the world.

The basic spiritual meaning of baptism is to die to the old self and to rise to new life in Christ. It is to experience salvation, or, to use the words of Paul, justification before God and reconciliation with God. We are baptised without the use of water by the Holy Spirit into the Body of Christ: we are born again (John 3). We are incorporated into a true communion with God and into the Christian community. This is the beginning of discipleship.

Learning based on teaching is the process of becoming disciples. The task is not an easy one, for the teaching is not just mere facts or repetition of the truths of Christianity but a teaching which begins a learning process with the goal of obedience to God. It is one of the essentials that the Christian Church has stressed throughout its history. It is possible to neglect this urgency in teaching and learning to our great loss. We stress the experience of salvation, of the initiation into Christ, but sometimes do not teach the skills of a life of discipleship. To be obedient to the Great Commission we must make sure these skills are taught and learned. We learn by the example of others and the most powerful teaching we can give is coherence between the lives we live and the witness we give.

The mission statement concludes with, 'I will be with you always.' This reflects the words from Isaiah 7:14 that are quoted in Matthew 1:23: 'They will call him Immanuel – which means, "God with us". The one who has all authority in Heaven and on earth is the one who promises the immediate presence, the comforting and empowering presence. 'Therefore' (on the basis of the presence) 'go and make disciples!'

Mission as practical deeds

Our original Salvationist mission call, 'saved to save', has over the years come to be matched by its counterpart phrase, 'saved to serve'. It describes the fullness of our mission expressed in the phrase 'heart to God and hand to man'.

Matthew 25:31-46 illustrates this concept of mission. The everyday episode which Jesus uses is that of the shepherd, each night separating the sheep from the goats. The goats are sent to a cave where they can be kept warm during the night, while the sheep need fresh air and are kept in a fold in the open.

Jesus turns this picture into an image of judgment. The separation is not based upon believing or not believing, but on compassion in action and lack of both compassion and action. It is a very strong image of judgment, which forces us to consider the basic values of our Christian commitment and mission, and how these values are brought into action.

The parable speaks of six concrete actions of love, three to do with the basic human needs of food, drink and clothing and three social needs, which are met by companionship, compassion and identification in vulnerable situations. To be in mission is to care about these needs and to transform our compassion into action. It is presented as a whole package, as if to say that the basic human material needs cannot be separated from the social needs. Our response to them must be a response to all. Secular charitable giving for the relief of basic human need is not identical with Christian compassion or mission in action. We must put our hearts and souls into it, feeding the hunger of individuals for fellowship and compassion as well as meeting their physical needs.

Mission as preaching

The primary command of mission is to be witnesses and to preach the message of salvation. True disciples of Jesus take to heart these words: 'What I tell you in the dark, speak in the daylight; what is whispered in your ear, proclaim from the roofs' (Matthew 10:27).

There are many words in the New Testament which describe preaching – proclaim, announce, teach, explain, speak, say, testify, persuade, confess, charge, admonish. This variety allows everybody to make a personal contribution towards the fundamentals of mission – the preaching of the Word. It reflects the different gifts we have and the different ways in which people hear the Word and are able to receive it.

Believers must always be concerned about the Word and pray for the success of the Word. 'Finally, brothers, pray for us that the message of the Lord may spread rapidly and be honoured, just as it was with you' (2 Thessalonians 3:1). Karl Barth expresses this centrality of the preaching of the message of salvation in this way:

> 'By Jesus' commission the apostles were sent out into the world in order to attest to all men that Jesus is this Word of God. Once again, the subject and strength of their commission were neither their impression of Jesus, their estimation of his person and his work, nor their faith in him. Instead, their theme was God's mighty Word spoken in Jesus' resurrection from the dead which imparted to his life and death, power and control over all creatures of all time. The apostles spoke, told, wrote, and preached about Jesus as men who were in this way directly illumined and instructed. They spoke as men who had behind them the empty tomb and before them the living Jesus' (*Evangelical Theology: An Introduction*, page 29).

There is an urgency to share the gospel that permeates the New Testament. We see it in the mission of Philip, Stephen, Peter and Paul and in local communities such as Thessalonica. 'The Lord's message rang out from you not only in Macedonia and Achaia ... your faith in God has become known everywhere' (1 Thessalonians 1:8).

Mission as dialogue

In John 4:1-42, in the story of the meeting between a Samaritan woman and Jesus at the well, we have an illustration of how a disciple is made through the means of dialogue. It starts with a meeting where the walls of convention are broken down. There was every reason why this woman should not be approached. She was a Samaritan, she was a woman and she was a 'fallen woman'. But these reasons were not considered valid. Jesus simply ignored these barriers.

In this setting a dialogue takes place, which is characterised by encounter and change. It begins with a simple request, a cup of water. They are at the well and the woman has come to draw water, so that would be a natural opening of a dialogue, apart from the fact that social convention forbade approaching a woman of that kind. The request leads to an encounter between the two, where the woman uses disarming humour to ease the uncomfortable situation. The response of Jesus reveals his mission. He reveals that he knows her identity and her social status, that he knows of her fallen life. Still he is in dialogue with her. This is the beginning of the change in the woman, a change that makes her a witness.

It shows that true dialogue, where we listen and try to find common ground, is an effective way to mission. Dialogue is not a one-way communication, it is an interchange that changes those engaged in it. It is a powerful tool in mission.

Mission as crossing boundaries: the mission principle of Paul

In 1 Corinthians 9:19-23 Paul shares his principle of mission with the church in Corinth: 'Though I am free and belong to no man, I make myself a slave to everyone, to win as many as possible. To the Jews I became like a Jew, to win the Jews. To those under the law I became like one under the law (though I myself am not under the law), so as to win those under the law. To those not having the law I became like one not having the law (though I am not free from

God's law but am under Christ's law), so as to win those not having law. To the weak I became weak, to win the weak. I have become all things to all men so that by all possible means I might save some. I do all this for the sake of the gospel, that I may share in its blessings.'

Paul understood that the gospel of Jesus is intended for all without distinction. Because of that he had a sense of responsibility to all, or a deep obligation – 'I am bound both to Greeks and non-Greeks, both to the wise and the foolish' (Romans 1:14). 'I am compelled to preach. Woe to me if I do not preach the gospel!' (1 Corinthians 9:16). His obligation was not a burden, but an act of gratitude. He saw it as a privilege.

It is an amazing statement with far-reaching consequences for us. We must also keep in mind that the gospel is intended for all and therefore reaches out to all. What Paul is stating is that in mission we identify ourselves with people. We find the points of identity or the common ground which can be recognised. We have a long Army history of identification with others to draw upon for inspiration. It requires the ability to suffer with and to rejoice with. In Matthew 9:36 Jesus shows this ability: 'When he saw the crowds, he had compassion on them, because they were harassed and helpless, like sheep without a shepherd.'

Paul gains his mission principles from Christ, whose 'model of mission' is stated in Philippians 2:6-11: 'Who, being in very nature God, did not consider equality with God something to be grasped, but made himself nothing, taking the very nature of a servant, being made in human likeness. And being found in appearance as a man, he humbled himself and became obedient to death – even death on a cross! Therefore God exalted him to the highest place and gave him the name that is above every name, that at the name of Jesus every knee should bow, in heaven and on earth and under the earth, and every tongue confess that Jesus Christ is Lord, to the glory of God the Father.'

This is our focus. Our privilege stems from here, a privilege expressed in mission as an act of gratitude.

Mission of hope

Our mission is built on hope in God, on a promise of a reality which is yet to come: 'Grace and peace to you from him who is, and who was, and who is to come' (Revelation 1:4).

We keep this hope alive because we believe, 'that the power of the gospel of Jesus Christ constantly proves to be stronger than all human incapacity and superficiality, stronger than our own sloth, folly and discouragement' (Hans Küng: *On Being a Christian*, page 529).

Our mission of hope is particularly important in places and at times where hope seems to have turned into hopelessness or is contradicted by stark realities. Hans Küng describes mission in such circumstances: 'Particularly in a phase of stagnation the important thing is to endure and hold out in confident faith. Opposition can be expected. But there is no real renewal without struggle. It is essential therefore not to lose sight of the goal, to act calmly and resolutely and continue to hope for a Church which is more committed to the Christian message and which is then more open, more kindly, more credible – in a word, more Christian' (*On Being a Christian*, page 529).

Václav Havel, who for many years was a dissident in Czechoslovakia, has given this explanation of what he considers hope to be: 'Hope is not the same as optimism, neither is it a certainty that something will succeed. It is the assurance that something has meaning in spite of whatever might come.'

* * *

For group discussion

1. Discuss what you consider to be the most effective mission method in your situation.

2. What sort of cultures are dominant in your community? How do they affect mission by local Salvationists?

3. In this section hope is central. Hope is at the heart of our worship, we are called to be a community of hope, and we are given a mission of hope. Discuss what Christian hope is – and to what extent Christian hope is the 'motor' of genuine worship, true fellowship and effective mission.

SECTION TWO

THE MINISTRY OF GOD'S PEOPLE

Introduction

THERE are three primary and indispensable foundations to the ministry of God's people: a theology of vocation, a biblical theology of priesthood, and a theology of the gifts and fruits of the Holy Spirit. These three inseparable concepts are rooted in biblical theology and have been developed during the theological history of the Church. Therefore, they are all fundamental to our understanding of ministry.

We recognise the central truth in all of these dimensions of the ministry of God's people. We are called to offer our ministry as praise and thanksgiving for the gift of salvation in our daily lives. This is part of our worship in the world. In daily life we are able to offer spiritual sacrifices, as we are reminded in 1 Peter 2:5: 'You also, like living stones, are being built into a spiritual house to be a holy priesthood, offering spiritual sacrifices acceptable to God through Jesus Christ.'

Such sacrifices include prayer, praise and thanksgiving; but they also include penitence, justice, kindness, love, the knowledge of God and the urge to share in the sufferings of this world.

We believe that the proclamation of the gospel by all possible means is the same for the whole of God's people, but that the performance of our ministry differs. Some ministries, such as that of preaching, are public. Other ministries, such as keeping financial records or carrying out secretarial duties, are more private and hidden.

Some people are called to the ministry of leadership, which takes on many forms – the service of planting, building up and leading corps; the service of overseeing the work of the church; the service of guaranteeing purity of faith by the teaching of the Word. Such diverse ministries are part of any fellowship of believers which, however small in numbers, nevertheless is the Body of Christ on earth, Christ's Church, and everyone in the fellowship can glory in that reality.

Chapter Four

VOCATION

THERE is a danger in many branches of Protestantism, including The Salvation Army, of developing a notion of vocation that is more linked to historic Roman Catholic teaching than Protestant teaching. As we will see, the implication developed in Roman Catholicism was that the genuine vocation (calling) from God was to holy orders, while the vocation of the laity was second best in the eyes of God and the Church. In the Army we must carefully avoid any assumption that the only true vocation within Salvationism is the divine calling to be an officer, or that not being an officer is sort of second class. Our shared calling to be soldiers of the Army is from God and equal to all other callings to serve the Saviour. All callings are empowered by the same divine grace.

Vocation in the New Testament

In contrast to the Jewish rabbi who had students coming to him to ask for permission to follow him, Jesus called his own followers (Mark 1:16-20). He did not call them to exclusive studies, but to a way of life and an attitude towards life that he demonstrated. When he called 12 disciples they represented the 12 tribes of Israel and thus were a witness to the fact that Jesus desired to call the whole people of Israel back to God. But Jesus also ministered to Samaritans and Gentiles as well as Jews, to the sick as well as to those who did not need a physician, to women as well as to men, thus reminding us that the way of the gospel is a way which calls all people to Christ.

Such calling likewise elevated all daily vocations to which people were called, because now there was a recognition that such vocations came from God and could be lived out to the glory of God. So Paul continued as a tent maker even after his Damascus road experience, and Peter continued his vocation of fishing after he was called to preach.

However, the followers of Jesus immediately recognised that Jesus' primary proclamation was that the Kingdom of God was at hand, and he manifested the coming of that Kingdom in many ways: through his teaching, through his healing, through his casting out of demons and through his praying. Jesus described his own ministry as one of service. He said, 'For even the Son of Man did not come to be served, but to serve, and to give his life as a ransom for many' (Mark 10:45). 'For who is greater,' Jesus asked, 'the one who is at the table or the one who serves? Is it not the one who is at the table? But I am among you as one who serves' (Luke 22:27). At the time of the Last Supper Jesus said, 'Now that I, your Lord and Teacher, have washed your feet, you also should wash one another's feet. I have set you an example that you should do as I have done for you. I tell you the truth, no servant is greater than his master, nor is a messenger greater than the one who sent him' (John 13:14-16).

Jesus' ministry of service culminated in offering his whole life for the reconciliation of the world. That ministry of service and reconciliation he has passed on to us, and he calls all believers into such ministry (2 Corinthians 5:18-20). And this ministry may be demonstrated by various means in the vocations to which God has called us.

Vocation in the Church

The institutional church, however, failed to maintain the strong connection between ministry and vocation. Medieval Christianity separated the temporal and the everyday from the spiritual and the eternal. The church saw the laity as having temporal authority, but no authority in the spiritual realm. Because the spiritual realm was deemed superior to the temporal, those in holy orders were assumed to be superior to the laity, and therefore their vocation – their calling from God – was also deemed to be a superior calling to which all genuinely committed Christians would respond. Lesser Christians, either unable to respond because of marriage and family responsibilities, or unwilling to respond because they felt no sense of calling to holy orders, had to resign themselves to their inferior Christian status and to their inferior secular vocations.

The reformer Martin Luther coalesced a reaction against this kind of false teaching by the Church and addressed both of these issues in his passion for restoring to the Church a genuine biblical understanding of Christian life. His theology joined together what the Church had sundered – the spiritual and the temporal – and thereby broke down the wall of separation between those two. God had not so ordered the world at creation, but had seen all of his creation as good and worthy. This vision of God still prevails. There is sanctity to all creation.

Luther began addressing the notion of vocation by reminding his hearers and readers that all Christians are called first to God and then to daily means of living out one's faith in the world in response to God's love and in service to God. The distinction between the sacred and the secular, what Luther referred to as 'pure invention', is broken down because all vocations are equally worthy, and all vocations serve the ministry of the Church. Luther used the examples of household chores and common labour to drive home this biblical principle, and in a work written in 1520 entitled *The Babylonian Captivity of the Church* he stated that, 'The works of monks and priests, however holy and arduous they may be, do not differ one whit in the sight of God from the works of the rustic labourer in the field or the woman going about her household tasks, but ... all works are measured before God by faith alone ... Indeed, the menial housework of a manservant or maidservant is often more acceptable to God than all the fastings and other works of a monk or priest, because the monk or priest lacks faith.'

Luther and others combated the prevailing religious notion that had developed over hundreds of years of Christian history that working in the everyday world was demeaning and degrading and the common labourer or the common household worker was therefore an inferior human being. Alister McGrath has written in his *Reformation Thought: An Introduction* that, 'All human work, however lowly, was capable of glorifying God. Work was, quite simply, an act of praise' – a potentially productive act of praise.' Work was done for the sake of the world but was ultimately a way of glorifying God. No work was intrinsically secular, but an individual secularises work when it is done in disregard for God and his creation.

It is interesting that Luther's doctrine of vocation was ultimately lodged within his understanding of sin. David Wells in his *No Place for Truth; or Whatever Happened to Evangelical Theology?* goes to the heart of this matter with the following statement:

> *This radical reshaping of religion by the Protestant Reformers produced the basis for a new social order, although it took some time for this to be worked out. There was at the centre of the Reformation gospel a new egalitarianism built upon the foundation not of self-evident natural rights (as in the American Constitution) but rather of common and equal loss – the loss of righteousness and standing before God. It is because no one has any claim on the grace of God, because in sin all stand on the same ground together, that no one can claim to be elevated over anyone else in society on the basis of some hidden, divine order. The most obvious and tangible outworking the Reformers gave to this belief, interestingly enough, had to do with vocation ....*

With such a grand vision of God's created order and of our part in it, and with the knowledge that all vocations are equally worthy, Luther could assure believers that they are equal in the eyes of God.

This is what Mark Noll in his book entitled *Turning Points: Decisive Moments in the History of Christianity* called 'a theory of spiritual democracy'.

Vocation in today's Church

We immediately recognise that this doctrine of vocation does not in any way deny that some are called to the specific ministerial tasks of preaching, teaching or administration. Nevertheless, we also gladly affirm that the doctrine of vocation acknowledges that all believers are in ministry. Our ministry is to proclaim the glorious gospel with urgency and in whatever way we can through our lives and through our words. We proclaim because we have encountered the Word and are bound to Jesus Christ and his rule, and having received the Spirit of God we confess Jesus as Lord and live out that confession in our daily lives.

Regardless of the nature of the vocation to which God has called us, all vocations, all ministries, are 'diakonia' service. Such service must take body and shape in ministry that seeks the lost to such an extent that it bears the signature of Christ, who presented himself as the one who serves. Hans Küng in *On Being A Christian* reminds his readers that: 'The sign of a true vocation is not a miracle, but service for the benefit of the community.'

Likewise, we are constantly reminded that our service is in solidarity with each other. Küng also wrote: 'Any kind of ministry in the Church therefore is of its nature dependent on solidarity, on collegial agreement, on discussion among partners, on communication and dialogue.'

We are dependent upon each other because we live out our ministry not primarily as individuals, but as a fellowship of brothers and sisters who stand equally in their vocations before the one God who forgave us of our sins and called us by his grace. Our joint ministry builds on tasks given to us and on the gifts of grace to accomplish those tasks. The first book of Peter 4:10, 11 states: 'Each one should use whatever gift he has received to serve others, faithfully administering God's grace in its various forms. If anyone speaks, he should do it as one speaking the very words of God. If anyone serves, he should do it with the strength God provides, so that in all things God may be praised through Jesus Christ.'

It is of critical importance, therefore, that we recognise and value this understanding of the vocation of all. Our vocations are genuine callings from God the Father and we follow those vocations freely and joyfully in obedience to God himself. The hope is that all Salvationists would recognise what Henri Nouwen calls 'an inward imperative' in their lives and would follow that imperative to the glory of God.

* * *

For group discussion

1. What is the biblical vision for an understanding of vocation?

2. How can we affirm that all vocations are equally worthy?

3. How does a Christian's daily work enhance the Kingdom of God?

Chapter Five

PRIESTHOOD

THE second important idea in this discussion is biblical teaching about the priesthood, which helps in breaking down the false teaching that there is a distinction between the sacred and the secular. All believers serve by God's grace as priests to one another.

Priesthood in the Old Testament

In the Old Testament the priests had two basic functions. The first was to maintain the institutions of Israel. This was done through teaching the law and its implications for living, offering sacrifices and preserving the worship life of the community. The second function was mediatory – to represent the people to God. The priests acted as the community's representatives in offering sacrifices for sin and pleading to God on behalf of the people. Priests were recognised as spiritual leaders, enjoying a special place in the life of Israel and supported by the nation because of their distinctive responsibilities.

The concept of priesthood was not used only of those who shared the priestly calling. There was a broader theological foundation to that concept. Indeed, in Exodus 19:5, 6 Moses envisaged the whole people of God, Israel, as fulfilling the priestly office. 'Although the whole earth is mine, you will be for me a kingdom of priests and a holy nation.' Years later the prophet Isaiah proclaimed, 'And you will be called priests of the Lord, you will be named ministers of our God' (61:6). The whole people of God, not only the Levitical priesthood, were set apart for the worship and service of God. All were endowed with the special status and that accompanied the responsibilities of intercession and ministry, without detracting from the reality that some were called specifically to minister as priests in temple worship. Such a vocation was never intended, however, to give those priests any privileged place in the community. They had no more special a status in the eyes of God than the Israelite performing the lowliest service.

However, this universal priesthood of Israel was not confined to the formal worship of God in the tabernacle or the Temple, nor was it confined to service around religious rituals. Such priesthood embraced the whole of life, extending through human relationships to the care for all of God's creation. Isaiah envisioned this development in such a way that it included the responsibility of taking God's salvation to all the peoples. God speaks to Israel in Isaiah 49:6, saying, 'It is too small a thing for you to be my servant to restore the tribes of Jacob and bring back those of Israel I have kept. I will also make you a light for the Gentiles, that you may bring my salvation to the ends of the earth.' This broader understanding of the priesthood would be carried over into New Testament theology.

Priesthood in the New Testament

The New Testament uses the idea of the Jewish priesthood in two ways: in connection with the work of Christ, and in connection with the ministry of God's people. With the destruction of the Second Temple in AD 70, the formal vocation of the priesthood was discontinued. The traditional priesthood, with its ritual significance, was set aside and Judaism developed as an internal religion, emphasising a life of prayer, meditation and study. However, the imagery of the priesthood was still significant to the writer of Hebrews who stressed that for Christians there is only one high priest, Christ himself. 'Therefore, brothers, since we have confidence to enter the Most Holy Place by the blood of Jesus, by a new and living way opened for us through the curtain, that is, his body, and since we have a great priest over the house of God, let us draw near to God with a sincere heart in full assurance of faith, having our hearts sprinkled to cleanse us from a guilty conscience and having our bodies washed with pure water' (10:19-22).

The New Testament Scriptures affirm that there is now no need for a separated, intercessory priesthood standing between the Lord and the reception of his grace.

All believers have immediate access to that grace through Jesus Christ. The great 16th century reformer, Martin Luther, called this 'the priesthood of all believers', meaning that each believer comes before God as his or her own priest, not needing any human intermediary. Also, all believers can assure each other that God's grace is readily available by being priests to each other within the Christian community, serving each other, interceding for each other and assuring each other of the forgiveness of sins and the availability of the sanctifying power of the Holy Spirit. Indeed, we are enjoined to, 'Carry each other's burdens, and in this way you will fulfil the law of Christ' (Galatians 6:2).

Again, the Scriptures command us to, 'Confess your sins to each other and pray for each other so that you may be healed' (James 5:16).

This mutual priesthood within the Christian community is to be extended to the world. In 1 Peter 2:4-10 Peter builds on the prophetic passage in Exodus 19. His argument is that this prophecy has been fulfilled in the new people of God, the Church. As a Body, the Church is God's holy priesthood. It is the focus of worship, holiness, prayer and sacrifice. Its priesthood is to be exercised individually only as part of the whole, for the calling of God is to be fulfilled corporately as 'a chosen people, a royal priesthood, a holy nation, a people belonging to God' (v. 9). The priesthood is Christ's, and ours only as we are members of Christ's Body.

This New Testament understanding of priesthood had serious implications for the ministry of the whole people of God. Although the authority of Jesus' teaching ministry was recognised by his disciples (they commonly called him rabbi), there was in that Jewish world no clear-cut division between clergy and laity, along with the implications that clergy were more spiritual and the laity less so. In manner, speech and mood Jesus identified himself as a servant, and often carried out ministries which today in some churches are called lay ministries. Likewise, the disciples, whom we might call the laity, were at times commissioned to preach.

Priesthood in the Church

Unfortunately, the Church as it developed did not remain faithful to this biblical understanding of priesthood. The Church came to distinguish sharply between clergy and laity, between religious and secular vocations, and the reformers could find no scriptural ground for that development.

With his emphasis on the priesthood of all believers, Luther freed laypersons to pray for themselves and each other, counsel each other and teach each other. These were indispensable aspects of priesthood for Luther.

In the 18th century, John Wesley's class meetings provided invaluable weekly opportunities for believers to act out the doctrine of biblical priesthood in these intimate ways. Indeed, the genius of the Wesleyan class meetings was that a small group of believers could meet together each week to provide time for the people of the church to minister to each other. No priest is needed for such ministries. No ordained authority is needed for these tasks. The whole Body of Christ is called to this ministry and the biblical theology of priesthood provides the theological foundation and legitimacy for such ministry.

'Through baptism,' Luther wrote in his treatise *To The Christian Nobility of the German Nation*, 'all of us are consecrated to the priesthood.' There is no sacred world in which priests minister and no secular world in which laypersons minister. All of God's creation is sacred and all Christians work as priests in that creation, especially in ways mentioned above.

However, great care must be exercised at this point. It is important to note that Luther, while holding to the doctrine of the priesthood of all believers, contended that not all Christians could or should hold the 'office' of priest. Not everyone is capable of carrying out the vocation of the priest. That is a different issue from the priesthood of all believers. As Alister McGrath has said in *Reformation Thought: An Introduction*, 'The recognition of the "quality" of all believers thus does not imply the "identity of all believers".' He states:

> *Nevertheless, not everyone could be allowed to 'act' as a priest. Luther's doctrine of the priesthood of all believers did not entail the abolition of a professional ministry. Luther's fundamental principle was that all Christians share the same priestly status on account of their baptism; they may, however, exercise different functions within the community of faith, reflecting their individual God-given gifts and abilities. To be a minister is to stand alongside one's fellow Christians, sharing their status before God; nevertheless, those fellow believers have recognised the gifts of that individual, and invited him or her, directly or indirectly, to exercise that ministerial function amongst them.*

Luther himself said: 'Although we are all priests, this does not mean that all of us may preach, teach and exercise authority. Certain ones from within the community must be selected and set apart for such office. Anyone who holds such an office is not a priest by virtue of that office, but is a servant of all the others, who are just as much priests as he.'

Two points are worth noting here. First, the doctrine of the priesthood of all believers, while acknowledging that we are all priests, has never meant that we can all publicly minister and teach.

Second, it is always critical to affirm that those who hold the ministerial office are not superior to other Christians. They, like all of us, are servants of Christ.

Priesthood in today's Church

As with the doctrine of vocation, so it is with the biblical doctrine of priesthood which must be linked in today's Church, including The Salvation Army of today, to our ministry and mission. Only then will we understand the foundation for ministry, as well as the outworking of the biblical approach to priesthood. This provides the basis for our understanding of Christian ministry. Ministry and mission are closely linked. We are called into mission through our ministry, and our ministry builds on the task of mission. In 1 Peter 2:9-10 we are told of the closeness of ministry and mission: 'But you are a chosen people, a royal priesthood, a holy nation, a people belonging to God, that you may declare the praises of him who called you out of darkness into his wonderful light. Once you were not a people, but now you are the people of God; once you had not received mercy, but now you have received mercy.' We are a chosen people, a royal priesthood. We are all in ministry. We are God's chosen people to be in mission.

Priesthood belongs to all true believers and is basic to membership in the Christian community. The core of that ministry is to declare the praises of God. Such praises are possible because every ministry is based solely on God's grace and the mercy which we have received from God.

In Romans 15:15, 16 Paul rejoices in 'the grace God gave me to be a minister of Christ Jesus to the Gentiles with the priestly duty of proclaiming the gospel of God'. Paul experienced the debt of sin being taken away and being transformed into a debt of gratitude which he expressed in his ministry. Such priesthood is derived from Christ. We are priests as he is Priest, children of our Heavenly Father and participators in the glorious Kingdom of Christ.

In John 21:15-19 Peter was given the task of shepherding the followers of Jesus, thus underlining the fact that grace and mercy are the foundation of any ministry. Peter had denied Jesus, but in this account he is restored to ministry by a forgiving response to his denial. Ministry is based on God's grace and not on human merit.

Priesthood belongs to all Christians because of their close and direct contact with Jesus Christ. The images which we find in the Gospel of John underline this closeness: the images of the shepherd in 10:11-18, of the grain of wheat in 12:24 and of the vine in 15:1. Neither sheep, grain nor branch needs a mediator nor can be a mediator, for each receives its life directly from the one shepherd, the one root or the one vine.

Ministry is shared throughout the whole priesthood of God. This does not mean that every aspect of the priestly ministry is evidenced in every person. Rather, ministry is exercised as individuals receive and use their natural abilities and spiritual gifts for the benefit of all, as will be shown in the next chapter. Every gift glorifies God and can be used in his service. This biblical understanding of priesthood, along with a theology of vocation, allows for and indeed prizes the preaching and teaching of the gospel.

Moreover, such understanding also recognises with gratitude that some are granted the gift of leadership and the call to leadership that carries with it a certain authority and that equips others to offer their gifts in service to Christ and to the world. The constant danger, of course, is that those with the more public abilities, such as preaching, teaching or administration, may assume some special status or privileged place. Such thinking negates the servant ministry to which they are called, jeopardises the New Testament teaching of ministry, fails to call people to obedience to our Lord, who himself became a servant for us and for our salvation, and endangers the New Testament doctrine of priesthood.

Biblical priesthood is corporate rather than individualistic, and is likewise based on servanthood rather than on arbitrary authority that fails to recognise the equality of all vocations. It is imperative in today's Army to embrace a biblical theology of priesthood. This is inextricably linked to the concept of vocation that we discussed in the previous chapter as well as to key teaching on the gifts and fruits of the Holy Spirit, to which we now turn.

* * *

For group discussion

1. Why is the biblical concept of priesthood important?

2. How may we serve as priests to one another?

3. What opportunities are given in the life of the corps for small groups of believers to come together and minister to each other?

Chapter Six
SPIRITUAL GIFTING AND SPIRITUAL FRUITS

ONE of the most important ways of describing Christian believers is as 'the people of God', the 'laos' in New Testament Greek. It is a term that describes without exception all of us who have been brought together by our response to the call of God and by the life-changing effect of his grace in our lives (1 Peter 2:9, 10). All God's people are called to be disciples, that is, to follow Jesus. Discipleship is not optional for Christian believers. We are called out from the world to be part of a special community of faith whose life takes its character from the risen Lord.

By this calling, we are ministers of the gospel (2 Corinthians 5:18). That is, we, like our Lord, are servants of God's grace. We have experienced the forgiveness of sins and the offer of new life, through the gift of the Holy Spirit (Acts 2:38). The gift of the Spirit's presence and power enables us to enter into a new and loving relationship with God, the relationship of grace.

Along with the transformation of our characters come the Spirit's gifts to share with and enrich the whole Christian community. The gifting of the Holy Spirit is the third important foundation for the ministry of the whole people of God. Just as all Christians have a vocation to ministry and all are priests of God to one another and to the world, the Spirit's gifts are given to all believers. Christians receive the Holy Spirit when they are born to new life in Jesus Christ. And it is the same Holy Spirit who works within them, producing the fruits of Christlikeness and, at his own initiative, distributing gifts to be shared with the whole Church.

Paul uses two words to describe these gifts. In 1 Corinthians 12:1 he uses the word 'pneumatika' which is translated 'spiritual gifts' in the *New International Version* of the Bible. The Spirit is the source of the gifts. In 1 Corinthians 12:4 and Romans 12:6 he speaks of the gifts as 'charisma' (from 'charis' – grace.). They are gifts of God's grace, that we have received in the new life.

Every new Christian brings new wealth to God's Church. It is in and through the Church – that is, the community of God's people, the Salvation Army corps – that Christians exercise their spiritual gifts. We are the Body of Christ, made up of many parts. Each of us contributes the gift or gifts we have received from the Holy Spirit towards the life and health of the whole body (1 Corinthians 12).

The grace of God is his self-giving love towards us which changes the relationship between us, while the gifts the Holy Spirit confers upon us are the means by which the love of God can flow between the people of God and out into the world. It is this giving and receiving of gifts which contributes to the special nature of Christian fellowship and mission. We enter into a new relationship of knowing and loving one another as God's grace is shared among us.

The gifts of the Holy Spirit are necessary to equip the people of God for their ministry to one another and for their mission to the world.

Spiritual gifts strengthen the Church's fellowship. We are urged to 'excel in gifts that build up the Church' (1 Corinthians 14:12) and reminded that gifts are given 'so that the Body of Christ may be built up' (Ephesians 4:12). It is in our corps fellowships first and foremost that we need to hear and respond to the gospel message. We should give each other help in time of need, and grace and mercy offered unconditionally. In these ways the Body of Christ is nurtured and grows strong. There are many examples of corps and churches unable to share Christ's message with the world because as a body they are starved of the essential nurture that the exercise of spiritual gifts can bring.

Spiritual gifts are also given so that the Church's witness and ministry can be strong. Some gifts are specifically evangelical: they endow those who receive them with special ability to proclaim the gospel in ways that others can hear and receive. Some gifts draw people into the fellowship of the Church so that they come within the range of the gospel message. The purpose of gifts is 'to equip the saints for the work of ministry' (Ephesians 4:12, *New Revised Standard Version*).

Spiritual gifts also help to define the particular form of ministry that each person can give. The gifts are distributed to individual Christians, not equally, but according to the Spirit's will and purpose, so that all God's people may be blessed. It is therefore essential for all Christians to discover their spiritual gifting, so that they can contribute to the movement of the Spirit in the world. This can be done through prayer and reflection, through sharing with others, through continued obedience to God and through listening to the Holy Spirit, who speaks to us in his many languages.

Salvation Army soldiership has always included the essential understanding that every Christian is involved in ministry and mission. The Salvation Army soldier is saved in order to further the mission of God in the world. All Salvationists should be encouraged to discover and use their own gift or gifts in whatever way the Spirit directs.

However, at this point, before the gifts of the Holy Spirit are further discussed, it is essential to say that there is an even more central matter to be highlighted for all believers. It is the place the 'fruit of the Spirit' have in each believer's life and spiritual development. In Galatians 5:22, 23 we find a list of the Christlike qualities that form the character of the authentic follower of Jesus. Whereas each believer receives at least one gift of the Spirit and cannot expect to receive them all, it is very different when we learn about the fruits of the Spirit. Each is a way of being like Jesus. None is an optional extra. Every Christian should have all the fruits in their life, to one extent or another. The more mature a Christian is, the more evident these things will be. The gifts can be simulated, but the fruits cannot. The gifts are about what we can do in service for God, but the fruits are about whether or not we are like Jesus in our inner and outward being. The latter is the much more important topic for every believer. It makes little sense to ask 'What can I do?' before I ask 'Am I like Jesus?'.

Old Testament understanding

Our understanding of spiritual gifts has its origin in the Old Testament. Here there are several places where the particular presence of God with an individual is marked by the gift of God's Spirit. In the early histories, the 'Spirit of the Lord' rested, for example, upon Bezalel (Exodus 31:2, 3), upon Gideon (Judges 6:34), upon Saul (1 Samuel 10:10), upon David (1 Samuel 16:13). Those who received the Spirit were given special powers for particular purposes. Bezalel was given the gift of craftsmanship to build and beautify the tent of meeting. Others, like Gideon, were given gifts of leadership, especially courage in the face of enemies.

The Spirit also fell on many other unnamed prophets, gifted with the power of ecstatic utterance. Their activities sometimes had to be tested or curbed because of the danger of false or demonic manifestations. 'Test the spirits' is a necessary caution in the Old Testament as well as the New (for example, Deuteronomy 13:1-5; 1 John 4:1). The latter prophets were especially gifted with 'the word of the Lord' (for example, Jeremiah 1:4-10), as their messages changed the face of Israel's spiritual understanding. Some of these prophets, like Joel, began to look forward to a time when the Spirit of God would come with power on all people (Joel 2:28-31).

New Testament teaching

The Old Testament does not speak of the Holy Spirit or his gifts with New Testament understanding. The old dispensation knew nothing of the Pentecost experience. The Spirit was given to the few for specific purposes, his presence could be withdrawn as well as bestowed, his person was only dimly defined. Then came Jesus, the man perfectly filled with the Spirit, who promised his disciples that they, too, would receive the Spirit (John 14:16-17) as his gift. Those who experienced the coming of the Holy Spirit with power at the first Pentecost had been informed by the expectation created in the pages of the Jewish Scriptures (Acts 2) and by the words and work of Jesus. The Holy Spirit, who now filled all present with new power, had been given so that all who put their trust in Jesus Christ could receive him. The gift of the Spirit was to be universal, not just for the chosen few.

This transformation of individuals by the power of the Spirit resulted in the creation of the community of believers that became the Church. The new Christians praised God publicly together, met in fellowship together, prayed together and shared their possessions with one another. In Acts, the apostles are clearly identified as the leaders of the Church in its earliest days, but, as the Church grew, the apostles, or the Spirit directly, harnessed the gifts of others in evangelism and mission, in service to the Church and in special ministries of encouragement or of prophecy. It soon became evident that the Spirit was enabling a wide variety of people to contribute to the ministry of the Church. With the gift of the Spirit came his gifts.

The New Testament letters, written during the time of rapid growth of the infant Church, contain various lists of the Holy Spirit's gifts in a number of well-known passages. The main ones are Romans 12:3-8, 1 Corinthians 12:1-11, 27-31, Ephesians 4:7-12 and 1 Peter 4:7-11. The lists should not be regarded as exclusive or exhaustive. They describe 'different kinds of gifts' (1 Corinthians 12:4). They refer specifically to the various manifestations of the Spirit current in the early Church. There is no reason to think that they were intended to limit the Holy Spirit's special gifts to those particular needs. While many of the gifts identified in these sections remain essential for today's situation, the Spirit is the Lord of the present and the future and continues to equip the people of God for ministry that is relevant to every age.

The lists in 1 Corinthians 12 include the gifts of wisdom, spiritual knowledge and potent faith. They are gifts that are especially relevant to the needs of a growing, young church, such as the church at Corinth in the first century, though by no means limited to that time. In such a period of dynamic activity, the Spirit provides God's people with the necessary abilities to encourage growth and guard against self-delusion and false direction.

The lists in Romans 12 and 1 Peter 4 include some of the same gifts as 1 Corinthians, for example prophecy, and also simple and practical gifts, such as generosity to others, mercy and hospitality. The terms are not used to describe any kind of hierarchy or ministerial status. They are simply given to enable all of Christ's people to minister to one another in Christ's name. There are also some references to leadership gifts in these passages.

Paul in his writings does not seem to distinguish between the more charismatic gifts, such as miracles or healing, and those less public, such as helping (for example, 1 Corinthians 12:28). Some gifts may be 'natural' in the sense that they relate to our natural disposition or talents. These, too, are spiritual gifts, not just given by the accident of birth, but enhanced and redirected through our spiritual rebirth. When our whole being is brought more and more into the sphere of God's grace, a process of transformation takes place through the work of the Holy Spirit, so that natural abilities, which could be used for good or ill, are directed towards the service of Christ and his mission.

The five New Testament passages mentioned above help us to understand the nature of spiritual gifts. The Holy Spirit is the initiator of all of Christ's gifts. 'There are different kinds of gifts, but the same Spirit' says Paul in 1 Corinthians 12:4, reminding us that, whatever gifts we or others may receive, they come from the same source (as also verse 11).

Paul carefully adds, 'There are different kinds of service, but the same Lord' (verse 5). The Holy Spirit is the mediator of the gifts of Christ – he does not work or speak independently. 'He will not speak on his own; he will speak only what he hears, and he will tell you what is yet to come' (John 16:13; see also John 16:14, 15; Ephesians 4:7, 8).

Unity and diversity

While all gifts are given 'for the common good' (1 Corinthians 12:7), there is both unity and diversity in the way in which spiritual gifts are bestowed. Each Christian receives at least one spiritual gift (1 Corinthians 12:7; Ephesians 4:7). In that sense there is no distinction among Christians. We are all in ministry with gifts appropriate to the service Christ asks of us. However, all have different gifts (1 Corinthians 12:4; Romans 12:6). This is our diversity in ministry.

Some gifts are spectacular, though they are not necessarily the most important (1 Corinthians 12:21-26). In Romans 12 and 1 Corinthians 12, Paul uses the famous analogy of the body to illustrate this unity and diversity (Romans 12:4-5; 1 Corinthians 12:12-31). In diverse ways the Spirit enables members of the one Church to serve each other and the world. Each member plays his or her part so that the Body of Christ may be whole and fruitful. Love, the greatest gift of all (1 Corinthians 13:13; 1 Peter 4:8; Romans 12:9-10), enables each to serve the other without pride or envy, but with humility and objectivity (Romans 12:3).

Such diversity can be, and has been, the cause of dissension and disharmony among Christians. Some have tended to exalt one or more of the gifts above others, some have expected certain gifts to be evident in those holding particular offices. Some Christians have recognised certain gifts as Spirit-given, but not others.

Wayne Grudem, in his chapter on spiritual gifts, makes this comment:

> *We should be willing to recognise and appreciate people who have gifts that differ from ours and whose gifts may differ from our expectations of what certain gifts should look like. Moreover, a healthy church will have a great diversity of gifts, and this diversity should not lead to fragmentation, but to greater unity among believers in the church. Paul's whole point in the analogy of the body with many members is to say that God has put us in the body with these differences so that we may depend upon one another (Bible Doctrine, page 399).*

All spiritual gifts are gifts of service (1 Peter 4:10) because they arise out of our relationship with God and with one another in Christ. Christ 'did not come to be served, but to serve, and to give his life as a ransom for many' (Mark 10:45). This is the ministry of Christ. He lived and died for us. So in serving one another we participate in that ministry and share the life of Christ with one another and with the world. As part of the Body of Christ, we belong to one another (1 Corinthians 12).

Spiritual gifts are given and used, then, in the context of that servant ministry. The New Testament urges us to offer our lives sacrificially to God as Christ gave himself for us, to regard ourselves and our abilities with humility and to use our gifts diligently. We are reminded to recognise the gifts of others and to receive them thankfully, to acknowledge that we are recipients of God's grace, that our gifts come from him and are determined by him. We are servants of others because we are servants of Christ (Romans 12).

Spiritual gifts as so described should determine our specific ministry rather than our place or status within a church or Salvation Army corps. 'If a man's gift is prophesying, let him use it in proportion to his faith. If it is serving, let him serve; if it is teaching, let him teach' (Romans 12:6-8).

'Where lists of ministries are given, these do not describe different offices or orders within the church, but give examples of the different functions which the Spirit, through distinctive 'charisms', enables to happen' (J. Tiller in *New Dictionary of Theology*, edited by Ferguson and Wright).

Gifts of leadership

Ministry, exercised through the gifts of the whole people of God, is the task of the whole Church. This is clear from looking at these early New Testament passages. It was expected that each person exercise his or her ministerial gift for the benefit of all. The picture that we see, especially from 1 Corinthians 12-14, is of a community structured in the round, with no visible hierarchical order. People contributed to the Church's life and worship, using their gifts as they felt led and with minimum direction.

There was the potential for disharmony and even chaos in this charismatic situation as the relevant chapters indicate. And yet the Church was not leaderless. Paul himself asserted his authority as an apostle of Jesus Christ and a guardian of Christ's specific will (see 1 Corinthians 14:37) to condemn disorder and to urge the Corinthian congregation to focus on their common mission under Christ. Paul exercised the gift of leadership given to him when he responded to the call of Christ on the Damascus road (Acts 22:14). Apostleship is one form of spiritual leadership found in the New Testament.

There are other models, too, that emphasise the importance of spiritual gifts. The clearest biblical pattern for gifts of leadership is found in Ephesians 4. Here, Paul speaks of the risen Christ, who 'gave some to be apostles, some to be prophets, some to be evangelists, and some to be pastors and teachers, to prepare God's people for works of service, so that the body of Christ may be built up' (Ephesians 4:11, 12). The variety of gifts is carefully described. Not all leaders are blessed with all the gifts (see also 1 Corinthians 12:28), but taken together they can describe the various functions that are desirable in the shared leadership of a church.

Exactly what Paul meant by each description is not entirely clear. For example, he is specific that only some are apostles. The word comes from the verb 'apostellein', meaning 'to send', and there is a sense in which all Christians are sent out by Jesus to fulfil the mission of the Church (see Introduction to Chapter 3). However, Paul clearly has a more specific ministry in mind here. Perhaps he is thinking of the Twelve, or more likely of all those who in the early Church were set apart by their congregations to take the gospel to new areas and to set up and lead new churches (see, for example, Romans 16:7). The prophets were those who exhibited the particular gift of discerning and interpreting God's Word with contemporary relevance.

Evangelists were those who had a special gift for preaching the gospel, especially to those outside the Church. Pastors and teachers had the gifts necessary for nurturing and training the Body of Christ in the faith.

According to this passage, all these gifts of leadership were to be used to enable the members of the Church to fulfil their callings as the ministers or servants of the gospel. It is this enabling function that is so important in the leadership of the servant Church. By their preaching and teaching, their care for others and for the needs of all, leaders help to foster the gifts of their whole congregations, encouraging growth and participation in all ministries. This must include encouraging others to take leadership roles as the Spirit directs.

Servant leadership is best shown when authority is used, not to dominate others, but to empower them.

Quenching the Spirit

Later New Testament writings, especially the Pastoral Letters, describe the beginnings of the institutional organisation of bishops, presbyters and deacons around which the government of the Church was to be developed. By the second and third centuries, groups of churches were in the pastoral care of bishops, and priests exercised ministry within individual congregations. Gradually the Church developed institutions of government and, throughout its subsequent history, the freedom and spontaneity of Spirit-led ministries were to be increasingly sidelined.

This did not prevent revivalist and charismatic expressions from breaking out, from the Montanists in the second century to the early Quakers and beyond, but on the whole the institutional rather than the charismatic aspect prevailed throughout the Church.

Medieval Catholicism did, however, encourage some religious practices that could be described as counterfeit spiritual expressions, more akin to magic than true spirituality, practices that drew people away from a saving knowledge of Jesus Christ. The reformers, especially John Calvin, rightly reacted against these practices and also against radical versions of Protestantism. In addition, they rejected the revival of apostolic gifts and taught the 'cessationist' doctrine, that the gifts described in 1 Corinthians 12, for example, had died out with the apostles and were not intended to be revived within the Church. This approach characterised reformed Protestant thinking for many centuries.

Gifting in today's Church

The rediscovery and appreciation of spiritual gifts in the Church in recent years have been the special legacy of the Pentecostal movement which became so influential in the 20th century. Three 'waves' of Pentecostalism have been identified during that period.

The first has become known as the 'Classical Pentecostal Movement'. 'Pentecostals' in the modern use of that term date from 1901 in the city of Topeka, Kansas, in a Bible school conducted by American holiness teacher and former Methodist pastor, Charles Fox Parham. He taught, falsely, that the gift of speaking in tongues was a necessary sign of the 'baptism in the Spirit' which should follow conversion. It was not until 1906, however, that Pentecostalism gained worldwide attention through the Azusa Street revival in Los Angeles led by the African-American preacher, William Joseph

Seymour. The teaching of Parham and Seymour caused controversy among churches in the early part of the century and resulted in various Pentecostal denominations, the largest being the Assemblies of God.

The second 'wave' had to do with 'charismatic renewal movements'. In 1959, Pentecostal theology and practices began penetrating mainline Protestant churches, one of the first being St Marks Episcopal (Anglican) Church in Van Nuys, California. The Roman Catholic Charismatic Renewal movement was also part of this wave, beginning in 1967 among students and faculty of DuQuesne University in Pennsylvania.

The 'third wave of the Spirit', a phrase popularised in church circles by Peter Wagner, originated at Fuller Theological Seminary in Pasadena, California, in 1981. In the classroom teaching of John Wimber, the so-called 'signs and wonders' gifts of the Spirit were emphasised, at first causing a good deal of controversy at Fuller but then coming into a more moderate phase as Peter Wagner later used Wimber in his own class teaching. Wilber's Vineyard churches came from that wave, but other mainline evangelicals also began to move more intentionally into spiritual gifts teaching during this period. That included teaching on signs and wonders, but with many of those evangelicals choosing to avoid labels such as Pentecostal or charismatic.

The Pentecostal/charismatic movement, which has left its mark on all churches, emphasises the importance of the gifts of the Spirit, believing that the teaching of the New Testament is powerfully relevant to the Christian community today. It expects the life of a church to be largely directed by the discovery and exercise of spiritual gifts by the whole congregation. This has led to some unease within the Army, as in other Christian denominations, because of the wrongly perceived conflict between 'Spirit-led' ministries and the structures of Army government.

However, the charismatic renewal has not materially affected the structure of church government. Priests continue to minister in the Catholic and Anglican churches and ministers and pastors in

Protestant denominations. Leadership remains a key to the growth of the universal Church, however leadership is described. It is important, therefore, that leaders are identified as much by their spiritual gifting as by their holiness and their desire to serve God fully. Some Salvation Army officers who show particular abilities to 'prepare God's people for works of service' will preside over healthy, growing corps, where all those who love Jesus Christ are involved in ministry. Others will lead effective social service centres where all their staff are encouraged to care for the poor in Christ's name and enable them to progress both materially and spiritually. The rediscovery of spiritual gifting, challenging as it is, provides a significant key to identifying ways in which all of God's people can be involved in sharing the gospel.

The Fruits of the Holy Spirit

Some Christians fall into the error of becoming overly fascinated by the gifts of the Spirit. They forget that spiritual maturity is paramount. Christlikeness is always the priority. A clear beginning in the holy life, through the blessing of a clean heart, and then steady development into Christian maturity will be the key safeguard against this error. Therefore each new believer should be taught clearly, and more experienced believers regularly reminded, that it is unhelpful to seek to use the gifts of the Spirit on the basis of an unsanctified life. This is what was going on in the Corinthian church and Paul found it necessary to offer words of loving, but firm, rebuke and correction. Too much emphasis was being placed on the exercising of the gifts, while more basic needs of character, inter-personal relationships and spiritual deepening were being overlooked. This is still a constant danger.

The gifts are seen as useful for service and mission – and they are – but too often the fruits of the Holy Spirit (love, joy, peace, patience, kindness, goodness, faithfulness, gentleness and self-control) are mistakenly regarded as unconnected with mission and soul-saving.

They are treated as though they are to be privatised within each believer's personal walk with the Lord, when in reality they are equally essential for outreach and mission as are the gifts. The attracting power of a Christlike life, a life that reveals more and more of the nine holy qualities mentioned above, cannot be overstated. In fact, a believer with, say, only one gift can live a life of deep sanctity and closeness to Christ. That life will do more to influence others for Christ than will an unsanctified life in which more gifts seem to be exercised. Christlikeness always comes first.

When we think of the fruits of the Spirit it is better not to picture a bowl filled with fully ripe fruit, juicy and polished, begging to be picked up and eaten at the whim of the chooser. Think rather of a small bud or tentative blossom on a tree that will slowly but steadily grow and grow into the fullness and maturity of the finished product. The Holy Spirit will do this in our lives if only we will make room for him. It is the work of a lifetime. It is the absolutely essential foundation for effective service and witness.

* * *

For group discussion

1. How can Salvationists today best identify their personal spiritual gifts? What teaching and ministry is necessary to enable them to do so?

2. What spiritual gifts do you think are essential for leaders?

3. What spiritual gifts are evident in your corps? How do they help the mission? How are they being nurtured?

4. How do you notice the fruits of the Spirit in your fellow believers? Discuss the nature of each of the nine fruits listed in Galatians 5:22, 23.

SECTION THREE

THE LEADERSHIP OF GOD'S PEOPLE – ITS SCOPE

Introduction

BOTH the Bible and Church history witness to the importance of effective leadership in the Spirit-led Church. Leaders are needed to provide vision and a way forward, to give sound teaching, to encourage good order and to nurture and shepherd the flock. None of these functions is the sole concern of leaders, but they are so vital that they should be owned and guarded by those specially appointed.

Today, as always, The Salvation Army is seeking to serve the present generation. It needs to guard its leadership well, if it is to be a movement with a contemporary vision, rather than an institution with a glorious past. In this section, we look at the scope of leadership within The Salvation Army. Many Salvationists, both officers and soldiers, have a leadership role to play today. It is vital that we understand well the relationship of our distinctive roles and that we make the best possible use of all those within our movement who have leadership gifts.

Some leaders are responsible for providing the vision and inspiration that the Church so sorely needs. Those with strong gifts for inspiring others help to focus the Church on its mission; they are prepared to take initiatives, they are often people-centred and attract others to follow them. They are not always at ease within set structures, but their leadership gifts are essential if the Church is to move forward. Without them, the work of God fails through lack of a vision to meet contemporary need.

Some leaders are teachers. Sound teaching includes proclaiming the gospel and teaching the essentials of the faith to all who become disciples. It is necessary so that the purity and power of the gospel message is preserved, that false teaching is identified and rejected, that God's people grow in the faith and are themselves held faithful to their ministry and calling. Leaders must be responsible for ensuring that this vital ministry is undertaken. Teachers are very often good team builders, finding great joy in bringing out the best in others and developing their potential for ministry.

Leadership also involves establishing and maintaining good order. The Church has a corporate identity. It is not a collection of individuals acting in isolation, but it is the Body of Christ. The Salvation Army is an intentional community, with a particular mission to fulfil, anxious to demonstrate faith in Christ by open and positive witness and action. It is composed of those who choose to serve within its ranks. Mutual concern and common purpose should mark all of its activity – only in that way will the message be clear to those who need to hear it.

The Body of Christ is first and foremost relational. It grows and develops as people interact with one another, sharing their lives, their hopes, their faith and their spiritual gifts. People need to be cared for – to be nurtured in the faith, disciplined when they stray and shepherded through the various circumstances of their Christian pilgrimage. Leaders are responsible for the care of the Christian flock, though they are by no means the sole carers.

If there is a proper understanding of the gifting of God's people within The Salvation Army, leaders, both officers and others, will emerge to exercise their gifts. They will recognise the call of God to specific service, and they will know what direction this should take for them. Their call will be affirmed by the recognition of the whole people of God and the gifts of the Holy Spirit will equip them for service. A servant ministry, spiritual authority and the ability to release the gifts of others will mark their spiritual leadership. They may well have their own particular ministry gifts that develop as their ministry grows and is enriched by experience, but their main joy will be to enable others to discover, develop and deploy their spiritual gifts for mission and ministry.

Chapter Seven

COMMISSIONING

THE word commissioning indicates that someone is being sent on a mission. Therefore, it signifies a calling from God rather than some special status, and the assurance for those who are commissioned lies in that calling rather than in some privileged position. General Albert Orsborn poignantly reminds us of this in his song entitled 'Not unto us, O Lord':

> *We were that foolish thing*
> *Unversed in worldly ways,*
> *Which thou didst choose and use*
> *Unto thy greater praise,*
> *Called and commissioned from afar*
> *To bring to naught the things that are.*

Commissioning involves the appointment of certain people to specific tasks or offices. Such people have received and responded to the call of the Holy Spirit for a particular ministry, and the community of believers has consented to that call and confirmed it. However, commissioning is not the setting apart of particular people to a superior status or a separated life, neither is it purely a private response to God's call. Christianity is a very personal religion, but it is not a private religion. The whole Christian community shares in the divine appointment by recognising the validity of the call of the one so appointed, and thereby owns and affirms that call. That essential response is a constant reminder that commissioning is an activity of the whole Army.

Commissioning in the New Testament

In the New Testament God's people are appointed to specific tasks and commissioned by Christ for ministry in the world and in the Church. The *Revised Standard Version* of the Bible (*RSV*) has used the noun 'commission' or a form of the verb 'to commission' in some New Testament passages. Paul, for example, spoke of his own commissioning and the commissioning of other apostles in 2 Corinthians 1:21 when he said, 'But it is God who establishes us with you in Christ, and has commissioned us' (most translations use 'anointed' here). And again in 2 Corinthians 2:17 he states that, 'We are not, like so many, peddlers of God's word; but as men of sincerity, as commissioned by God, in the sight of God we speak in Christ' (several translations speak of having been sent by God).

In 1 Corinthians 9:17 he reminds his readers that he has been 'entrusted with a commission' (*RSV*), which carries the idea of being entrusted with the stewardship of the gospel, and an account will have to be given some day of that stewardship. The gospel is not his own, but it is God's gospel which has been placed in his hands. The *New International Version* here reads, 'If I preach voluntarily, I have a reward; if not voluntarily, I am simply discharging the trust committed to me.'

In the New Testament neither the appointment to a specific task nor the act of sending out implies a separated, privileged ministry. Commissioning can be said to be biblical only when it is seen as an action in which the whole community of faith, the whole Army, is involved under the guidance of the Holy Spirit. Such was the case with the commissioning of Barnabas and Saul at the beginning of Acts 13 for the first missionary journey. Acts 13:3, 4 reminds the reader of the beautiful combination of the work of God and the work of the believers in sending forth people for ministry. The third verse states that the people of the church at Antioch, 'after they had fasted and prayed ... sent them off'.

However, the next verse speaks of Barnabas and Saul being 'sent on their way by the Holy Spirit'. The Church recognises the call, the affirmation by the believers and the sending out. This is the biblical pattern for commissioning.

An example from Church history

In England, there was a sending out of lay preachers during the Wesleyan revival, as had already been true among people who had dissented from established church practice. John Wesley became convinced that lay preachers could be sent out for service because the mission of the revival demanded that such preaching take place. He could find no place in the Scriptures forbidding such preaching. Also, the movement of the revival caused many laypersons to begin commenting on the Bible and then preaching from the biblical texts, and so lay preaching, in a sense, became unavoidable.

However, Wesley was driven by the mission of the Church rather than by strict standards of church governance, some of which he disagreed with in any case. He was convinced that the call to mission was the driving force in New Testament Christianity, and it therefore had become the driving force in the Wesleyan revival of the 18th century.

The Christian Mission of William and Catherine Booth certainly followed in the path of Wesley, without the encumbrance that Wesley had of having to please the Anglican establishment. The Booths originally envisioned The Christian Mission as a force for salvation purposes and as a means of sending people back to the established churches. For that reason, it was quite natural that they used lay preachers. All who had the appropriate gifts were sent out to preach.

A prime example of that was Catherine Booth herself. She began preaching on Pentecost Sunday of 1860 because she knew that God had called her. Catherine Booth needed and received no ordination from any denomination to confirm that calling. Her confirmation came from the people to whom she ministered. Likewise, after the founding of The Salvation Army she was never commissioned as a Salvation Army officer. Her public preaching ministry continued unabated until a couple of years before her death. Catherine Booth was what many would term a lay preacher.

Another early leader of The Salvation Army, George Scott Railton, although he had become a local preacher among the Wesleyans before joining The Christian Mission, would nevertheless be considered a lay preacher. He was never ordained to ministry, and when the Mission was in need of preachers, he and others, including women, were sent out to save souls and raise up saints. The history of The Christian Mission and the early Salvation Army demonstrates that in a sense all were lay preachers sent out to accomplish the work of the gospel. Distinctions between the laity and the clergy would arise only after God transformed the early Christian Mission, founded in 1865, into a steadily more structured body known from 1878 as The Salvation Army.

Commissioning in The Salvation Army

Today in The Salvation Army we teach the biblical principle that all Salvationists are in ministry. While distinctions between soldiers and officers may at times be useful and appropriate, we recognise that all officers are first and foremost soldiers in the Army and that everyone in the Army is in ministry both in the context of his or her daily vocation and in the context of life in the corps.

In the Army we have an important aid to understanding in our use of 'commissioning'. We commission both officers and local leaders to their respective ministries. We believe that this practice is biblically sound.

The broader Christian Church appropriates the terminology of commissioning quite frequently, effectively making use of the biblical notion of setting people apart for ministry. Sometimes that ministry takes place within the confines of the local church and sometimes it involves going into the world for service on behalf of the Church.

Usually such ministries are for specific assignments and for fixed times. Some ways in which the practice of commissioning might develop in the Army are as follows:

First, we could extend our understanding of commissioning. We have traditionally commissioned bandsmen, songsters and local officers, but commissioning to ministry could encompass a much wider range of Army activities.

Second, the commissioning of people to ministry might more clearly emphasise a time frame for that ministry. Some of our people might be more available for ministry if they knew that they would be allowed to commit themselves to a fixed period for that ministry.

Third, the commissioning service should be public and should be a pronounced part of the meeting. This is very important if people are going to take their ministry seriously. All around the Army world the commissioning of cadets to officership takes place in the context of a public meeting, regardless of the number of cadets being commissioned. Guests are invited, programmes are printed, and sometimes large meetings are held in connection with such commissioning. Obviously the commissioning within a corps setting cannot take place on this scale, but should, nevertheless, be a significant public event. We are limited only by our imagination as to how we can make commissionings at the local corps level great events in the life of the corps as well as opportunities to further its mission.

Fourth, all the people of the corps could be encouraged to take responsibility for those being commissioned. Commissioning ceremonies provide ample opportunities for the soldiers and adherents of the corps to support those who are being commissioned, pray for them and uphold them in their tasks in any and every way possible.

Because commissioning ceremonies should be occasions for publicly affirming the mission of the local corps, the whole corps will want to take ownership for the commissioning service and for those commissioned.

The Army is committed to defining its mission and implementing Catherine Booth's principle of 'adaptation of measures' to accomplish that mission. When asked about the reason for the success of the Army Catherine Booth's consistent reply was that the Army was adaptable.

In that light, all Salvationists must be mobilised and creatively used to achieve the twin goals of evangelisation and service. They must be challenged to speak to the culture in appropriate ways without accommodating to that culture. This demands careful and deliberate training of all soldiers, and increasingly the training and employment of all Salvationists should become a high priority for the movement. The principle of adaptability demands that we become more creative in our thinking about commissioning our people to ministry.

The Church cannot fulfil its role in the world without the cooperative ministry of all the people of God, both clergy and laity, officers and soldiers. For too long passive laity and a clergy defensive of its status and role have inhibited the life and work of the Church. The Army wishes to avoid this danger at all times and in all places.

However, a word of caution is necessary here. Such statements can lead to an imbalance in another direction that devalues the role of so-called 'professionals' in the ministry of the Church. While the biblical doctrine of priesthood recognises the authority appropriate to every ministry, it also acknowledges the specific authority of those who are called and trained for ministries of preaching, evangelisation or administration. This recognition should not detract from a mutual regard for one another's ministries or weaken the desire that all should work together as one Body and as the people of God. All who belong to Christ serve as priests to each other and are likewise in service to the world.

The working together, therefore, is not only implemented by an emphasis on commissioning, but is nurtured and sustained by such an emphasis. We value the gifts and the abilities of those who are so commissioned, and rejoice because any commissioning to service, both the commissioning of officers and the commissioning at the local corps level, enhances the ministry of the Army and thereby the Kingdom of God.

The encouragement of public commissioning services in the life of the corps underscores this and reinforces the biblical understanding of the Church as the Body of Christ. Members of that Body are affirmed in their service in this very public way.

The three previous chapters dealing with vocation, priesthood and gifting have all emphasised that the whole people of God are called to ministry. The call for commissioning in this chapter does not negate the understanding that some are commissioned to the ministry of officership within The Salvation Army. Those who are commissioned to that office are also ordained to servant leadership. The next chapter deals with that critical subject.

* * *

For group discussion

1. How is the commissioning of an individual related to the community of believers?

2. Why should commissioning services be public occasions?

3. Relate commissioning to what has been discussed in the chapters on vocation, priesthood and gifting.

Chapter Eight
ORDAINED TO SERVANT LEADERSHIP

THE focus of this book, as indicated in its subtitle, is on the calling, ministry and leadership of all Christians. That approach is in accord with the chapter of *Salvation Story* entitled 'People of God' under the heading, 'The Holy Spirit empowers the whole Church for witness':

> *Our Christian pilgrimage demands an enduring commitment to a life of discipline and a tentative relationship to distracting world values. The Church is the community where Kingdom values are taught and lived, thereby encouraging us to sustain a radical lifestyle in keeping with our calling. We are called to live holy lives in the world and to see ourselves as set apart to be ministers or servants of the gospel. All Christians have direct access to God through the priesthood of Christ. All are called to exercise the challenging ministry of intercession on behalf of one another and for the world. In Christ, all Christians share in the priestly ministry. All vocations are important opportunities for expressing discipleship. In that sense there is no separated ministry.*

There is, however, another emphasis made in the final two paragraphs of that section:

> *Within that common calling, some are called by Christ to be full-time office-holders within the Church.*

> *Their calling is affirmed by the gift of the Holy Spirit, the recognition of the Christian community and their commissioning – ordination – for service. Their function is to focus the mission and ministry of the whole Church so that its members are held faithful to their calling. They serve their fellow ministers as visionaries who point the way to mission, as pastors who minister to the priests when they are hurt or overcome, as enablers who equip others for mission, as spiritual leaders.*

Full-time office-holders could include any believer, not exclusively clergy or Salvation Army officers. It is important that the ministry of clergy and laity, of officers and soldiers, is a shared one. While we speak of 'officers and soldiers' as a convenient distinction in terminology, it is fully recognised that all officers are soldiers (laity) first and foremost.

Soldiers of The Salvation Army are full-time ministers, but their service is usually undertaken in the world, in the course of a regular occupation, in the midst of family and social life. All are priests of God in a shared ministry of the one Body of Christ. All work together through the guidance of the Holy Spirit, each submitting to the other and enabling one another so that the work of Christ can be continued.

The term 'ordination' is, however, normally used specifically with reference to clergy or Salvation Army officers. This is in keeping with Luther's indication that certain ones from within the Christian community are selected and set apart for preaching and teaching and exercising authority within the Church.

Ordination in The Salvation Army

In The Salvation Army this does not mean that preaching, teaching and exercising authority cannot be part of the ministries of soldiers, but it emphasises that an ordination to spiritual leadership is especially integral to officership. Salvation Army officers are given authority to exercise their spiritual leadership by the call of God and the confirmation of the people.

A United Kingdom officer, Major Ian Cooper, in a paper entitled 'A Theology of Salvation Army Officership', has said:

> *It is important to notice that the making of an officer has two aspects. From one aspect the initiative is from God in the calling, equipping and sending forth of this minister. From another aspect the community has its own important part to play in the process. The Army must test the call of a candidate, discern the gifts of the Spirit in this person and receive what is a gift from the Spirit to the Church. It also authorises the officer to serve in a leadership capacity and is responsible for the welfare and ongoing training of the new leader.*

Officers are equipped by gifting as well as training and are prepared to offer themselves full-time for ministry, as mission leaders, shepherds of the flock, comforters, enablers of the ministry of those in their care. Like all involved in the priesthood of believers, they also have a priestly function as ministers of the grace of God to those who call upon them.

There are a number of questions concerning the ordination of Salvation Army officers. These arise because of comparisons with ordained ministers of the gospel in other denominations. One of those questions is whether the term 'ordination' is interchangeable with and of the same meaning as the term 'commissioning'.

Some say that would seem to be so in that there has been little or no change in the concept of officership since the introduction of the term 'ordain' as part of the commissioning ceremony for officers. Others say that the introduction of the term has changed the concept of both officership and our movement. They suggest that the term 'commission' is related to an Army with an outgoing mission. to the world, while the term 'ordain' is related to a commitment to an organisational 'church' structure. They would also suggest that the introduction of the term 'ordain' has furthered an Army mindset shift from mission to maintenance.

Terms are normally defined by actual experience. They depend on what meaning is given to them by the people of a movement. The caution provided by the above debate is, however, an important one. We must not forget the reason we were first called The Christian 'Mission'.

If terminology has an effect on reality, it may be important to maintain the use of both terms, as is the case today. Officers are commissioned to be missioners, and ordained for ministry in a movement that is a vital part of Christ's Body in the world of today, the Church of the living God.

Why was the term 'ordination' introduced into the commissioning ceremony? It would seem to have been introduced partially to facilitate an understanding of how solemnly the commissioning of Salvation Army officers is regarded and understood. An accompanying reason for its introduction was a desire within the Army that a Salvation Army officer be regarded as having a God-given office in every way as significant as that of a priest or minister or pastor ordained to ministry in any other denomination.

The early writings of the Army reveal a conviction that the Army had been raised up by God and was as truly a part of the historic Church as any other communion. William Booth claimed for the Army equal plenitude of spiritual authority, spiritual understanding and spiritual function to that of other churches. Bramwell Booth said: 'Of this Great Church of the Living God, we claim, and have ever claimed, that we of The Salvation Army are an integral part and element – a living fruit-bearing branch in the True Vine.'

It followed then that Salvation Army officers were believed by our early leaders to have as valid a ministry as leaders in other denominations. Bramwell Booth saw the methods of the selection of early leaders of the Army as similar to ways in which leaders were chosen and appointed to fulfil Christ's mission in the early days of the Church. He pointed out that there was then no priestly system but rather a freedom to meet the demands of a mission situation with such means as seemed best under the guidance of the Holy Spirit.

However, many churchmen did not admit those claims in our early history. Part of the reason for that had to do with our perceived lack of contact with the historic apostolic succession. In negotiations with the Anglican Church in the 1880s in its move to incorporate the Army within its structures, limited status and authority were being proposed for our leaders. It would seem that only by going through the procedure of apostolic validation at the hands of bishops would Army leaders have been put on an equal footing with their counterparts in the Church of England.

There are still a few church leaders who question the validity of the Army's place as an integral part of the Church of Christ. Some may fail to recognise Army officers as equivalent to other ministers of religion. These perceptions have, however, gradually changed since the early years of our history. The Salvation Army accepted an invitation to be associated with the International Missionary Council founded in 1921 and was a founding member of the World Council of Churches in 1948.

The Salvation Army today is recognised by church councils at all levels, from local to national through to international. We are part of the World Council of Churches, are an associate member of the World Evangelical Alliance, are represented on the International Lausanne Committee for World Evangelisation and have participated in the formation of such interdenominational bodies as the Great Commission Roundtable. Salvation Army officers are asked to represent the Army on national councils of churches, national evangelical bodies, local interdenominational councils and church-related conferences, and increasingly are requested to participate in ecumenical activities alongside ministers of other denominations.

It was believed by Salvation Army international leaders in the 1970s and 1980s that these signs of equivalence of standing with the ordained clergy of other churches might be aided by associating the historic Church term, 'ordain', with our traditional term, 'commission'. On 30 May 1978, the Chief of the Staff wrote to international leaders with the following advice from General Arnold Brown:

> *It is the General's wish that a slight modification should be made to the wording of the Dedication Service during the Commissioning of cadets, in order to emphasise the fact that Salvation Army officers are ordained ministers of Christ and his gospel. After the cadets have made their Affirmation of Faith, the officer conducting the Commissioning should then say: 'In accepting these pledges which you each have made, I commission you as officers of The Salvation Army and ordain you as ministers of Christ and of his gospel.' In countries other than English-speaking, and where the word 'ordained' has no exact equivalent, a translation should be used which will give the nearest possible meaning to the English-language expression.*

Following that advice, certain parts of the world questioned the use of the word 'ordain' when commissioning cadets. The following is an extract from the minutes of the Conference Implementation Commission meeting held at International Headquarters on Friday 18 October 1988, following discussion at the 1988 international leaders conference:

> ORDINATION: *The introduction of the word had been important for the USA where it was desired to manifest equal status with the ministers of the gospel. It had been helpful in India and generally accepted in Africa. However, in some languages no direct*

translation was possible. There were territories, particularly in Europe, where the use of the word caused some distress. Territorial leaders in such situations should be sensitive to the feelings of their people. Generally it was felt to be difficult to withdraw the use of the word. A warning was issued that ordination might be legally construed as 'ordination for life', making possible legal action against termination of officership in some instances.

The following recommendation was agreed:

The Commission recommends that the use of the word 'ordination' be confirmed. Any territorial variation deemed wise may be cleared through the international secretary with the approval of the Chief of the Staff.

That recommendation was confirmed in a letter of 28 April 1992 from the General to international leaders. General Eva Burrows indicated that the General's Advisory Council had considered the matter and made a positive recommendation, embracing previous statements. A memorandum by the Chief of the Staff, entitled, 'Commissioning and Ordination of Cadets', was attached to the letter, stating the following:

By the issuing of this memorandum it is confirmed that the word 'ordained' will remain as part of our commissioning ceremony. Therefore, after the cadets have made their Affirmation of Faith, the officer conducting the commissioning shall say: 'In accepting these pledges which you each have made, I commission you as officers of The Salvation Army and ordain you as ministers of Christ and his gospel.'

Should a variation to this rule be thought wise in a particular territory, a proposal should be submitted by the territorial commander/officer commanding to the international secretary for decision by the Chief of the Staff.

In 2008 a further minute by the Chief of the Staff was promulgated containing a comprehensive ceremony of commissioning and ordination of cadets in which the following choices were provided for the actual words of commissioning to be spoken to each cadet.

> *Recognising that God has called you, has equipped you and gifted you for sacred service, I now ordain you as a minister of the gospel of our Lord and Saviour Jesus Christ, and commission you as an officer of The Salvation Army with the rank of lieutenant.*

OR:

> *We rejoice that God has called you, has equipped you and gifted you for sacred service and therefore we now ordain you as a minister of the gospel of our Lord and Saviour Jesus Christ, and commission you as an officer of The Salvation Army with the rank of lieutenant.*

OR:

> *With gratitude to God for your calling into the paths of sacred service and for his empowering and gifting in your life, you are now ordained as a minister of the gospel of our Lord and Saviour Jesus Christ, and commissioned as an officer of The Salvation Army with the rank of lieutenant.*

The full minute can be seen at the end of this chapter. The decision having been made to retain the term 'ordain', a further question has to do with ways in which the ordination or commissioning of Salvation Army officers relates to the ordination of clergy in other denominations. We will begin by exploring biblical and historical perspectives.

Ordination from a biblical perspective

In the Old Testament tradition, priests and kings and prophets were particularly consecrated and ordained and anointed for ministry. Moses was instructed by God to put special clothing on Aaron and his sons to give them dignity and honour and then to anoint and ordain and consecrate them so that they might serve as priests representing the people before God (Exodus 28:41). Saul was anointed by Samuel to be king over Israel, since kingship too was considered a religious function and a ministry under God (1 Samuel 10:1). The Lord told Jeremiah that he had been set apart and appointed as a prophet to speak the word of the Lord to the nations even before he was born (Jeremiah 1:5).

In the New Testament age, Jesus Christ himself becomes the fulfilment of the consecration to the offices of priest, king and prophet that occurred in the Old Testament era. He is called by God to be a priest for ever (Hebrews 5:6), a great high priest who sacrificed himself for our sins (Hebrews 7:27). He accepts the title king of the Jews (Matthew 27:11). He indicates that the prophecy of Isaiah is fulfilled in himself as he has been anointed to preach good news to the poor (Luke 4:18).

The New Testament indicates further that all of Christ's followers are part of his royal priesthood (1 Peter 2:9), able to have direct access to God (Hebrews 10:19-22), offering him the sacrifice of praise and being involved in ministry for others (Hebrews 13:15, 16).

But involved in that consecration of the whole membership of Christ's Body there is our Lord's special choosing of the apostles for ministry (Mark 3:13-19), and through them the ordination of others for special purposes. For example, the seven men chosen to wait on tables in Acts 6 were set aside for special work (Acts 6:6). Paul and Barnabas were set apart and sent off for missionary service by the church at Antioch (Acts 13:3). Timothy was set apart by the apostle Paul to fan into the flame of ministry the gift of God which was in him (1 Timothy 4:14; 2 Timothy 1:6).

Ordination and commissioning of officers in The Salvation Army

In The Salvation Army, a cadet becomes an officer through commissioning and ordination. In the process, there are three components similar to those of the traditional Protestant doctrine of ordination to ministry.

The Three Spiritual Steps in the Commissioning of an Officer:

1. **The Officer Covenant**

The Officer Covenant is signed by a person about to be commissioned and ordained. The Covenant is made between that person and God. It is the means whereby a person binds himself or herself to God in the making of solemn vows.

The signing is done in the setting of a Covenant Service usually held in the chapel of the training college a few days before the commissioning and ordination meeting, in the presence of fellow cadets, training college staff, and territorial leadership. A senior officer witnesses the signature of the cadet in order to verify the signature, not in order to make the Army a party to the Covenant which, as said above, is between the cadet and God alone. It is the entering into a deeply spiritual relationship with God for sacred service of a specific nature.

The Bible has many examples of believers entering into sacred covenants with God, who accepts our covenants and takes them seriously. Each person signing the Officer Covenant does so of their own free will, in the clear understanding that the commitment is intended to be life-long: 'Called by God to proclaim the gospel of our Lord and Saviour Jesus Christ as an officer of The Salvation Army I bind myself to him in this solemn covenant to love and serve him supremely all my days.... Done in the strength of my dear Saviour....' (See *Orders and Regulations for the Training of Salvation Army Officers*, Chapter 8, Section 3).

2. ***The Commissioning and Ordination***

The Commissioning and Ordination meeting allows the wider membership of the Body of Christ to gather in order warmly to affirm and encourage those about to become officers, and in order to witness publicly the moments of commissioning and ordination.

The cadets are helped by the prayers and intercessions of the faithful. The cadets declare before many witnesses that they will be loyal to Christ, will hold to the Doctrines of the Army, will be available to the marginalised, and will be obedient to the principles and purposes for which God raised up The Salvation Army. (See *Orders and Regulations for the Training of Salvation Army Officers*, Chapter 8, Section 4).

3. ***The Appointing***

The Appointing is a public occasion when specific responsibilities are placed upon the newly commissioned and ordained officer. The officer is publicly granted the authority both to serve and to lead within the ranks of the Army. This is the outward authentification of an inward summons from God, and the imparting to the officer of the obligation to be a servant of all for the sake of Christ.

Note that in territories where the cadets are informed of their appointments before the commissioning and ordination meeting takes place, a public appointments meeting should still be held and the appointments given in a formal and public setting. It is important not to minimise this final spiritual step in the process by which a person becomes an officer of the Army.

The uniqueness of Salvation Army officership

In keeping with our tradition of not drawing rigid lines between officers and soldiers, it has been one of the distinctives of The Salvation Army to believe that there is no essential ministry exercised by a Salvation Army officer that could not also be carried out by a soldier. In some countries, legal ceremonies, such as that of uniting a couple in marriage, might be considered an exception to that principle, but these are exceptions only because of state constraints and not because of Salvation Army belief.

What then is unique about a Salvation Army officer? How does commissioning and ordination to Salvation Army officership differ from Christ's call to all Christians to be involved in Christian ministry? There are a number of possible responses to that question. They have to do with an authority of office in terms of the officer's relationship to the movement, the expectations of the movement towards the officer, decision-making powers related to finances, property, and worship leadership and availability. The officer has a particular function to be a focus for the mission and ministry of the Army. He or she is responsible through life and by ministry to ensure that the Word of God is proclaimed and the grace of Christ is offered in all possible ways to a needy and suffering world.

In other communions of the Church the distinguishing characteristic for clergy is being set apart for the ministry of the Word and Sacrament. At least in terms of function, there are ways in which the Salvation Army officer is also set apart for such ministry.

The officer has accepted the call of God to spend his or her life in proclaiming the Word of God in a variety of ways, so that all people might respond to that Word and become part of the community of those who are won from sin to Christ. The officer's covenant states: 'Called by God to proclaim the gospel of our Lord and Saviour Jesus Christ as an officer of The Salvation Army, I bind myself to him in this solemn covenant to love and serve him supremely all my days, to live to win souls and make their salvation the first purpose of my life.' The officer is therefore called to be a minister of the Word.

Because of the historical and God-given position of The Salvation Army with regard to the outward observance of sacraments (we are called to role-model sanctity without sacraments), there are some difficulties in seeing a Salvation Army officer as a minister of the sacraments. However, the Army accepts a theology of Christ as the one, true, original Sacrament. The International Spiritual Life Commission Report of 1998 said: 'Christ is the one true Sacrament, and sacramental living – Christ living in us and through us – is at the heart of Christian holiness and discipleship.'

Jesus Christ is the Sacrament received by the believer with gratitude and lived out in visible and tangible form through the sacramental living of his followers. All followers of Christ are called to this sacramental living. In signing their covenants, Salvation Army officers, particularly, accept the call to live the life of Christ, who is the one true Sacrament, in an exemplary and sacramental way as spiritual leaders in the Church of Christ and in the world, just as Christ called his first apostles for that purpose. Officers do so by pledging themselves 'to maintain the doctrines and principles of The Salvation Army, and, by God's grace, to prove myself a worthy officer'.

There is another paragraph in the revised officer's covenant of December 2000 that speaks of such sacramental living in very practical terms: 'I bind myself to him in this solemn covenant ... to care for the poor, feed the hungry, clothe the naked, love the unlovable and befriend those who have no friends.' This acknowledges that officership in The Salvation Army can lead to ministry in a wide variety of sacramental roles. One of the most significant is that of social service and social action.

The National Social Services Commission of the Army in the United States said this in a statement on the doctrine of social responsibility:

> *The Salvation Army's position is that Christian social responsibility is an imperative standing alongside evangelism, education, worship, and fellowship. The mission statement of The Salvation Army is clear and concise, 'To preach the gospel of Jesus Christ and to meet human needs in his name, without discrimination.'*
>
> *The Salvationist affirms that we are not saved only to enjoy our new life and to talk about it, but to do something with the new power and the benefits received – in word and deed to emulate Jesus. Indeed, it is through a perspective of seeing beyond ourselves that we fulfil the plan of salvation by extending unconditionally to those in need a hand of service, fellowship, and inclusion ... At the very heart of the gospel itself stands the manifesto of Jesus in Luke 4:18, 19 in which the gospel is defined in terms of proclaiming release to the captives, recovery of sight to the blind, liberating the oppressed, and proclamation of the jubilee. Compassionate meeting of human need and social action are fundamental to the gospel of Jesus Christ.*

Spiritual and servant leadership

The ministry of Word and Sacrament is essentially a ministry of spiritual leadership. This involves an officer's own spiritual life development and commitment to tasks that will aid the spiritual formation of others.

Orders and Regulations for Officers of The Salvation Army (1997) spells out the spiritual life development qualities of those called to officership in this statement:

> *By reason of the work to which they have committed themselves, and to which they declare themselves to be divinely called, it follows that officers must first of all live godly lives. This is a primary requirement for which neither physical energy nor natural gifts are any substitute. In the efforts to bring about a moral and spiritual change in the lives of others, an officer's personal godliness will count for more than any other quality. Abilities may arouse the admiration, even applause, of people but that which will create in them a desire for divine grace will be the example of a Christlike life.*

The call to lead others into similar spiritual life development by divine grace may be fulfilled in many different ways. In particular, that leadership may be in forms similar to those ministries outlined in Ephesians 4:11-13: 'It was [Jesus Christ] who gave some to be apostles, some to be prophets, some to be evangelists, and some to be pastors and teachers, to prepare God's people for works of service, so that the body of Christ may be built up until we all reach unity in the faith and in the knowledge of the Son of God and become mature, attaining to the whole measure of the fullness of Christ.'

When someone is ordained to such spiritual leadership, he or she is ordained to a ministry of servanthood to God and his world.

This applies equally to leadership exercised by officers and soldiers. Spiritual leadership and servant leadership are synonymous in the Church of Christ. Without spirituality, there is no servant leadership. Without a servant mindset, there is no spiritual leadership.

Dietrich Bonhoeffer in *Life Together* unites both of those qualities when he says:

> *The Church does not need brilliant personalities but faithful servants of Jesus and the brethren. The question of trust, which is so closely related to that of authority, is determined by the faithfulness with which a man serves Jesus Christ, never by extraordinary talent which he possesses. Pastoral authority can only be attained by the servant of Jesus Christ who seeks no power of his own, who himself is a brother among brothers submitted to the authority of the Word.*

It is not without significance that the term most often used for that to which one is ordained is 'ministry' in English. The term is derived from 'ministerium', which in Latin is defined as either 'office' or 'service'. This concept does not necessarily mean that someone ordained to the ministry of spiritual leadership primarily performs menial tasks. But when such menial tasks are called for, they are performed with the dignity of a servant leader.

Performing menial tasks willingly for others may indeed be a path to spiritual leadership. That concept is brought out in a book by Robert K. Greenleaf entitled *Servant Leadership: Journey Into the Nature of Legitimate Power and Greatness*. Greenleaf indicates that the idea of the servant as leader came out of reading Hermann Hesse's *Journey to the East*. In that story, Leo accompanies a party on a journey as the servant who does their menial chores, but who also sustains them with his spirit and his song. He is a person of extraordinary presence and all goes well on the journey until Leo disappears. Then the group falls into disarray and the journey is abandoned. They cannot make it without the servant Leo. The narrator, one of the party, after some years of wandering, is taken into the order that had sponsored the journey. There he discovers that Leo, whom he had known first as servant, was in fact the titular head of the order, its guiding spirit and a great and noble leader.

Greenleaf suggests that this story clearly says to him that the great leader is seen as servant first, and that simple fact is a key to greatness. Leo was actually the leader all the time, but he was servant first because that was what he essentially was. Leadership was bestowed upon a man who was by nature a servant. This principle is imbedded deeply in the teaching and example of Jesus. He said to his disciples, 'Whoever wants to become great among you must be your servant, and whoever wants to be first must be your slave – just as the Son of Man did not come to be served, but to serve, and to give his life as a ransom for many' (Matthew 20:26-28).

Our Lord enacted the principle of servant leadership throughout his whole ministry and even to his death on the Cross. It is a principle associated with his parable of the good Samaritan where love for others is equated with serving one's unlikely neighbour (Luke 10:25-37).

Servant leadership was particularly symbolised in the sacrament of the basin and towel when Jesus washed the feet of his disciples on the evening prior to the Crucifixion and said, 'I have set you an example that you should do as I have done for you' (John 13:15). This was a lesson from our Lord to his disciples that they were called to be servants. In the same way, the spiritual leader who is a servant most effectively serves his master and those to whom he ministers by mobilising others to be servants of the Lord through the Body of Christ. The Christian leader thus exercises his or her function as the servant of the servants of God.

The spiritual leader as servant recognises that all people of the Body of Christ have gifts in ministry to be developed and used in God's work. All persons in the Body of Christ therefore become ministers, with the one ordained to the ministry of spiritual leadership serving as a minister of the ministers of God. Spiritual leaders become enablers of the ministry of others, equipping others for spiritual service. They are therefore what Bramwell Booth called 'servants of all'.

* * *

For group discussion

1. What are areas of uniqueness about Salvation Army officership that you think are important? Discuss those areas mentioned in this chapter and add to them.

2. What do you understand by servant leadership? How do you encourage all persons in your part of the Body of Christ to be servant leaders?

2008/IA/08

MINUTE BY THE CHIEF OF THE STAFF

CEREMONY FOR THE COMMISSIONING AND ORDINATION OF PERSONS ABOUT TO BECOME OFFICERS OF THE SALVATION ARMY

The General has decided to authorise with immediate effect a new document entitled **Ceremony for the Commissioning and Ordination of persons about to become Officers of The Salvation Army**, a copy of which is attached below for your use.

CEREMONY FOR THE COMMISSIONING AND ORDINATION OF PERSONS ABOUT TO BECOME OFFICERS OF THE SALVATION ARMY

Issued by International Headquarters
On the authority of the General

1 April 2008

Officers authorised to conduct a commissioning and ordination ceremony

By virtue of their appointments or rank, only the following officers are automatically authorised to conduct a Salvation Army ceremony of commissioning and ordination:

1. The General;
2. The Chief of the Staff;

3. A Commissioner in active service;
4. A Territorial Commander.

Other active officers of appropriate rank or appointment, including an Officer Commanding, may conduct the ceremony with the prior written consent of either the Chief of the Staff or of the General.

No retired officer, however senior, may conduct a commissioning and ordination ceremony without the prior written consent of either the Chief of the Staff or of the General.

The General reserves the right, in exceptional circumstances, to appoint any officer to conduct a ceremony of commissioning and ordination.

General Information

1. Ceremonies of The Salvation Army should always be simple but dignified occasions. In the planning of any meeting that will include a formal ceremony, the overall aims should be those of:
   - honouring the Lord Jesus Christ;
   - seeking the conversion of those as yet unsaved;
   - building up believers in the faith;
   - giving opportunity for the making of first-time commitments to Jesus Christ or of further self-dedication for service to God's Kingdom in the Army.

A meeting that will include a commissioning and ordination as officers of The Salvation Army should always affirm those who have already responded to the sacred calling to be an officer, and should challenge others to accept that same life-long pathway of service if God the Holy Spirit is calling them to it.

2. The aims stated above should be followed even if the number being commissioned and ordained is not large.

3. A commissioning and ordination meeting is also an opportunity to deepen understanding of the life and work of the Army across the world, because reference can be made to the wide

variety of places in which officers serve and to the wide variety of roles an officer might be required to fulfil from time to time.

4. The Salvation Army does not teach that special or exceptional grace is conferred upon a person through the commissioning and ordination ceremony. We believe that the same divine grace is given to all who serve the Lord, regardless of status or capacity, and that such grace is available through simple faith in God and faithful obedience to his holy will.

5. Accordingly, The Salvation Army's commissioning and ordination of a person to become an officer is not for the receiving of special grace, but for good order in the Body of Christ, and for the carrying out of specific functions within the Army and therefore within the wider Body of Christ. For the same reason we do not regard a person as continuing to hold commissioned or ordained status in the event of his or her officership being terminated.

6. According to *Orders and Regulations for Officers of The Salvation Army* (Volume 1, Part 1, Chapter 1.1), an officer is defined as follows:

> 'Officers of The Salvation Army are soldiers who have relinquished secular employment in response to a spiritual calling, so as to devote all their time and energies to the service of God and the people and who, having successfully completed the required period of training, are commissioned as officers and ordained as ministers of the gospel of Jesus Christ.'

The words set down (see below), to be used by the officer conducting the commissioning and ordination, are based upon this definition and are consistent with it. They are also consistent with the ancillary definition of an officer stated in *Orders and Regulations for Officers of The Salvation Army* (Volume 2, Part 1, Chapter 7, Section 1).

7. The English word, 'ordain', carries both a wide and a narrow meaning. In its wider sense it means 'to decide' or 'to determine', for example as in the statement: 'God has ordained the heavens and

the earth.' The narrower, more specific meaning, is used when a person is made a minister of the gospel. It is in this sense that the word is used in the English language version of the Army's ceremony of commissioning and ordination. (In ceremonies conducted in other languages, the closest word to 'ordain' is to be used.)

8. The Army believes passionately that God constantly calls those whom he wishes to become officers, and that graciously he equips and empowers them for sacred service. It is the task of the members of the Body of Christ to recognise when a claim to having received a sacred calling is authentic, and then after suitable training and in the name of God to commission and ordain that person as an officer and therefore a minister of the gospel. Similarly, it is the task of those so appointed within the Army: a) to test and recognise when an authentic calling to officership has taken place; b) to admit that person for suitable training; c) to recommend that person for commissioning and ordination by the Army in the name of God.

9. The moment of both commissioning and ordination is when the officer conducting the ceremony speaks the appropriate words, as set down in the ceremony below, to the individual cadet in the presence of many witnesses.

10. Because a commissioning and ordination meeting is a high point in the life of all persons about to become officers, in the lives of their families, and also in the life of the wider territory or command, a suitably impressive commemorative brochure should be prepared. This can be used by the entire congregation throughout the meeting, and also retained as a precious and personal reminder of a sacred occasion. The words shown in *italics* in the ceremony below should be reproduced in the brochure for all to see.

11. Before the date of the commissioning and ordination meeting, the officiating officer should privately seek assurance that each cadet has recently signed the Officer Covenant and also the Officer Undertakings. The provisions set down with regard to the Covenant

and the Undertakings in *Orders and Regulations for the Training of Salvation Army Officers* (Chapter 8, Sections 1 to 3) should be carefully studied and observed, as should the instructions with regard to the Certificate of Salvation Army Officer Training (Chapter 1, Section 3, paragraphs 5 and 6).

12. The commissioning events are not training college events, but are territorial events. *Orders and Regulations for the Training of Salvation Army Officers* (Chapter 8, Section 4) refers to the need for good publicity and careful planning of the commissioning events which are among 'the territory's most important and significant events', with the respective roles of the training college staff and of the territorial leaders clearly stated. Training college staff will publicly participate in these events as appropriate and as decided by the territorial commander.

The Meeting

In addition to the formal ceremony itself, it is traditional to include the following aspects in a meeting for the commissioning and ordination of cadets:

1. Entry of senior leaders.
2. Entry of the Sessional Flag.
3. Entry of the cadets (referred to in the brochure by their Sessional Name) and of the staff of the training college, with the territorial commander and /or the officiating officer taking the salute from each cadet.
4. Explanation of the Sessional Name and its significance.
5. A short but warm-hearted mention by Sessional Name of the presence of the first year cadets supporting in prayer those about to be commissioned.
6. Lively congregational singing, prayers, and the reading of the Scriptures.
7. Personal spoken testimony by a cadet about to be commissioned.

8. Singing of the Sessional Song.
9. Reading of the General's Message.
10. A short, powerful Bible Message.
11. Presentation by the training principal to the territorial commander of the cadets, stating in public before many witnesses that they are ready for commissioning and ordination. This should immediately precede the commissioning ceremony itself.

Guidance on appropriate trimmings for the cadets:
During the commissioning and ordination meeting the cadets should wear cadet trimmings. Officer trimmings will of course be worn for the later appointments meeting. Every effort should be made to avoid the cadets wearing officer trimmings before they are actually commissioned as officers. Where the commissioning and ordination and the giving of appointments are not conducted in separate meetings, but are included in a single meeting, plans should be made for the cadets to leave the meeting briefly after being commissioned in order to change into officer trimmings and then make a formal re-entry, being greeted by the congregation, prior to the giving of the appointments.

The Commissioning and Ordination Ceremony

The officiating officer will remind the congregation of the sacredness and solemnity of these moments and will ask for a prayerful and dignified silence throughout.

Reference should also be made to the Covenant Service held in the days prior to the commissioning and ordination. The nature of the Officer's Covenant, by which persons about to be commissioned and ordained bind themselves to God, can be explained briefly (see Note 2 below). The wording of the Covenant can be reproduced in the commissioning and ordination brochure.

The congregation will be helped by an explanation (see again Note 2 below) of the three spiritual steps in the commissioning of

an officer of The Salvation Army. These are:
    The Signing of the Officer Covenant;
    The Commissioning and Ordination;
    The Appointing.

It is not appropriate to bring children of cadets forward or to the platform during a ceremony of commissioning and ordination.

Declaration of Faith by the Cadets

The cadets about to be commissioned and ordained say in unison:
In the name of God the Father, God the Son, and God the Holy Spirit, and in the presence of the officers, soldiers and friends of The Salvation Army here assembled, we declare that:

There then follow the words of the *Eleven Doctrines (Articles of Faith)* of The Salvation Army, each of which is to be said aloud unchanged by all the cadets in unison.

The officiating officer will say:
Do you promise faithfully to maintain and proclaim these truths?
The cadets will reply:
We do!
The officiating officer will say:
Do you regard it as your duty to bear this witness everywhere, to strive to lead all persons to their only Saviour, and for his sake to care for the poor, feed the hungry, clothe the naked, love the unlovable, and befriend those who have no friends?
The cadets will reply:
We do!
The officiating officer will say:
Do you promise by holy living, boundless charity and adherence to the principles and discipline of the Army to show yourselves at all times to be faithful officers of the Salvation Army?
The cadets will reply:
We do!

The officiating officer will say:
In the name of God I accept the declarations and promises you have made this day. We will now proceed to your commissioning and ordination.

The Commissioning and Ordination

Each cadet, including any married cadet, will step forward alone upon the calling of his or her name. Married cadets are officers in their own right and are to be commissioned and ordained as such. (For the giving of the first appointment in the Appointments Meeting, married cadets should step forward together, if they are appointed to serve together.)

Each cadet, wearing cadet trimmings, should also wear the Army colours (flag).

Each cadet will approach the officiating officer and give the Army salute which will be returned by the officiating officer before addressing the cadet.

Guidance on asking the cadet to kneel down:
In order to avoid any impression of submitting to merely human authority, it is better not to have a cadet kneeling down for the moments of commissioning and ordination. The Covenant has already been signed by the cadet as a first spiritual step, during the Covenant Meeting, in a kneeling attitude of prayer and obedience to God. Now, for the next spiritual step, an upright posture of readiness and availability is appropriate.

However, if the cadet is asked to kneel for those moments, this should not be done facing the officiating officer, but facing the congregation to signal submission to God in the presence of the people of God, and in order to avoid any impression that the officiating officer requires the cadets to kneel in submission before him or her.

Guidance on the 'laying on' of human hands:
The officiating officer should not seek to lay hands upon the cadets during the moment of commissioning and ordination. The ordination is carried out in the name of the Lord Jesus Christ whose hands were nail-pierced, and which no human hands can replace or supplant.

For the same reason it is not appropriate, as part of the commissioning and ordination meeting, for members of the congregation to place hands upon the cadets. Affirmation of the cadets by the congregation, if explicitly required, can be by many and varied other means such as prayer during the meeting or personal greeting at the meeting's conclusion.

No impression should be given that the 'laying on of hands' by any person is essential or required in order to grant ecclesial authority or ordained status upon a person. Note here paragraph 4 under General Information above regarding our teaching on grace. Officers receive the same grace, not special or additional grace, as a soldier or local officer and we do not 'lay hands' on making a person a soldier or local officer.

It is true that the New Testament sometimes refers to the laying on of hands when a person was set aside for a special task in the early church. The Army was raised up by God and exists today in a different historical setting, one in which many claim that a valid ordination to ministry requires the 'laying on of hands' as an essential ingredient. Some even claim that the hands used must be those of specific persons, such as a bishop, if 'apostolic succession' is to be upheld. Some even claim that the hands must be male hands.

It is important to understand that the Army does not hold any of these views, but sees spiritual authority for servant leadership as something that is imparted spiritually not physically. This is a key tenet of Salvationism and therefore the moment of commissioning and ordination is an ideal opportunity to give a powerful public witness to it by not using human hands.

Bible verses for each cadet and the words of commissioning and ordination:
The officiating officer is at liberty to read aloud a Bible verse, usually chosen by the staff of the training college for that particular cadet, addressing the cadet by name, and then saying with solemnity:

Recognising that God has called you, has equipped you and gifted you for sacred service, I now ordain you as a minister of the gospel of our Lord and Saviour Jesus Christ, and commission you as an officer of The Salvation Army with the rank of lieutenant.

OR:
We rejoice that God has called you, has equipped you and gifted you for sacred service and therefore we now ordain you as a minister of the gospel of our Lord and Saviour Jesus Christ, and commission you as an officer of The Salvation Army with the rank of lieutenant.

OR:
With gratitude to God for your calling into the paths of sacred service and for his empowering and gifting in your life, you are now ordained as a minister of the gospel of our Lord and Saviour Jesus Christ, and commissioned as an officer of The Salvation Army with the rank of lieutenant.

The officiating officer is free to use any of these three options throughout the ceremony, or to vary them from cadet to cadet. For the sake of good order and international consistency, no other verbal formulations are permitted.

When the words of commissioning and ordination have been spoken the officiating officer will affirmingly shake hands with the newly commissioned officer and present the Officer's Commission document. The newly commissioned officer will then return to his or her seat.

Prayer of Dedication

When all the cadets have been commissioned and ordained, a senior officer will offer a Prayer of Dedication, asking God to bless and seal the moments of commissioning and ordination, to guide and sustain the new officers, to use them for his glory, to help them mature in service, to bless their families and the people among whom they will serve in the days and years ahead. The prayer will include a petition that others will hear the call of God into the paths of officership and will find the grace and courage to respond gladly.

Notes

Note 1:
Local Cultural Practices:
It is recognised that local cultural practices of a Christian nature may, with the prior approval of the territorial commander, be required in some places as part of the commissioning and ordination meeting. These practices should be kept to a minimum, should be carefully controlled, and always be in keeping with the sacredness, dignity, and solemnity of the occasion. No local cultural practice must be allowed to change the wording, or the Army spirit, of the ceremony.

Note 2:
The Three Spiritual Steps in the Commissioning of an Officer:
1. **The Officer Covenant**
The Officer Covenant is signed by a person about to be commissioned and ordained. The Covenant is made between that person and God. It is the means whereby a person binds himself or herself to God in the making of solemn vows.

The signing is done in the setting of a Covenant Service usually held in the chapel of the training college a few days before the commissioning and ordination meeting, in the presence of fellow cadets, training college staff, and territorial leadership. A senior officer witnesses the signature of the cadet in order to verify the signature, not in order to make the Army a party to the Covenant which, as said above, is between the cadet and God alone. It is the entering into a deeply spiritual relationship with God for sacred service of a specific nature.

The Bible has many examples of believers entering into sacred covenants with God, who accepts our covenants and takes them seriously. Each person signing the Officer Covenant does so of their own free will, in the clear understanding that the commitment is intended to be life-long: 'Called by God to proclaim the gospel of our Lord and Saviour Jesus Christ as an officer of The Salvation Army I bind myself to him in this solemn covenant to love and serve him supremely all my days.... Done in the strength of my dear Saviour....' (See *Orders and Regulations for the Training of Salvation Army Officers*, Chapter 8, Section 3).

2. **The Commissioning and Ordination**

The Commissioning and Ordination meeting allows the wider membership of the Body of Christ to gather in order warmly to affirm and encourage those about to become officers, and in order to witness publicly the moments of commissioning and ordination. The cadets are helped by the prayers and intercessions of the faithful. The cadets declare before many witnesses that they will be loyal to Christ, will hold to the Doctrines of the Army, will be available to the marginalised, and will be obedient to the principles and purposes for which God raised up The Salvation Army. (See *Orders and Regulations for the Training of Salvation Army Officers*, Chapter 8, Section 4).

3. **The Appointing**

The Appointing is a public occasion when specific responsibilities are placed upon the newly commissioned and ordained officer. The officer is publicly granted the authority both to serve and to lead within the ranks of the Army. This is the outward authentification of an inward summons from God, and the imparting to the officer of the obligation to be a servant of all for the sake of Christ.

Note that in territories where the cadets are informed of their appointments before the commissioning and ordination meeting takes place, a public appointments meeting should still be held and the appointments given in a formal and public setting. It is important not to minimise this final spiritual step in the process by which a person becomes an officer of the Army.

Note 3:
Suggested Bible Readings:
Some suggested Bible readings for a commissioning and ordination meeting are:
Psalm 139
Isaiah 6:1-8
Isaiah 61
Jeremiah 1
Mark 1:14-20
Luke 10:1-20
John 13:1-17
2 Corinthians 2:14-17
Galatians 1:11-24
Ephesians 6:10-18
Philippians 2:1-18
2 Thessalonians 2:13-17
1 Timothy 3, 4

Chapter Nine
CONSULTATIVE MINISTRY

SERVANT leadership can be exercised in a variety of ways. There is a sense in which no single style has all the answers. Our early leaders often used a directive form of leadership which led to immediate action to deal with problems and needs, and which served the Army well in its formative stages. There are still benefits to that type of leadership when used appropriately. However, in many of today's cultural climates there is a broader ownership of decisions that are made when people other than the primary leader are allowed to contribute to the decision-making. In many cultures, the function of servant leadership may be fulfilled more effectively when the spiritual leader as an administrator and manager and visionary follows a more participative team management style of leadership.

It has been suggested that there are four basic styles of management: the dictatorial style, the authoritative style, the consultative style and the participative team style. Each style has value in appropriate situations and can be linked to the concept of servant leadership.

An authoritative leader, for example, can be a servant leader in a hierarchical system when there is a transparency to that system. In the participative team the ideal servant leadership style is the participative team style, leaders remain as team leaders, but members of the team are considered equal in terms of input and ideas. Leaders retain leadership responsibility as team facilitators, but they may choose to accept the team's ideas even when they disagree with their own. Such team leaders focus on stimulating creativity and innovation within the team, however time-consuming that may be in terms of team training.

Greater consultation and a widening of leadership responsibility have been evident for a long time in many areas of Army life. The consultation that is already in place, though, is poised to move further towards a more developed form of team ministry. This phrase has been used in the past to describe a particular form of officer leadership, where a group of officers takes mutual responsibility for several corps or centres. We seek models of leadership that enable the Army to work more effectively and creatively in the present world.

There is a need for change partly because of social factors. Many of us live in societies where formal authority structures and hierarchies are breaking down, or at least being strongly criticised. Social divisions between people are no longer so clear. The deference and respect for authority previously created by differences in race, gender and age matter much less. International governments, financial markets and intellectual and artistic disciplines are all affected by globalisation, which also breaks down familiar structures. Many people feel threatened by this cultural evolution and it is sometimes accompanied by understandably frightened protest, as different communities attempt to erect barriers to preserve their familiar world.

However, the changes are fundamental, and Christians preach a gospel that looks to the future. If our Christian ministry is increasingly open and inclusive, it will relate better to today's society.

In fact, the Church is already responding to social change, developing patterns of ministry and leadership that better reflect contemporary culture and that are fuelled by the theologies of vocation, gifting and the biblical concept of priesthood that we have already discussed. In some areas of Church life, this is leading to a startling growth in lay leadership. The rise and growth of the para-churches, with their emphasis on mission and their largely non-clergy leadership structures, is one example of multitudes of ministries led by lay people that are transforming the Church. This is true in The Salvation Army as well as elsewhere. In many places, soldiers are increasingly taking responsibility for mission initiatives, and there is a proliferation of different ministries reaching out to the unchurched and to those in desperate social need across the world.

In many cases, these ministries have a single focus and clear purpose, and they work on a model of team leadership that results in a creative synergy. They are energetic and productive. Their leaders display all the ministry gifts of apostle, prophet, evangelist, pastor and teacher, taking their places alongside officer-leaders as models of spiritual leadership and servant ministry. They can often serve the Church and the world in new and challenging ways.

A Trinitarian pattern

There is a sense in which these developments can be understood sociologically. Leadership in the Church needs to be understood theologically, as well as in the context of important social developments. Our whole life as Christians should try to reflect something of the nature of God, whose life invades and transforms our own.

How can consultative ministry be described theologically? One helpful way forward is in the context of a Christian understanding of God as Trinity. Chapter 2 of *Salvation Story* describes the relationship between the Three-in-One as follows:

> *God is never alone. Within himself he enjoys perfect and full fellowship. Although he is always three, he is not three individuals who could be in competition or opposition. He is three persons, always united in being, attitude and action, a threefold God of love ... Father, Son and Holy Spirit represent a dynamic circulation of life among equal persons without any authority or*

superiority of one over another. Any attempt to develop a false hierarchy of power and glory within the Trinity is to weaken the integrity of the Godhead and undermine the complete unity of the persons.

This picture could be a model for the mutual sharing of gifts as those called and gifted increasingly work together to lead God's people. While our human relationships can never hope to match the mutuality of the Godhead, the Spirit can work within us to create harmonious, life-giving action. It is the vibrant relationship of the persons of the Trinity that gives life and power: it can be the mutual sharing in ministry and leadership that creates the energy for vision and growth.

Such working together reflects the creativity of the Godhead. Both in our creation and in our redemption, we see how the mutual activity of Father, Son and Holy Spirit brings dynamic life out of what is bleak and barren. God also works with his people in the renewal and salvation of the world. In creation he calls us to play our part in caring for the world he has made. In his saving activity, he calls us to respond to his saving grace for ourselves and to share in his mission to the world. Consultative ministry, in a similar way, may be the most effective way of releasing the creative abilities of the Church. Certainly William Booth used his soldiers in such a way as to inspire and set free for initiative and service all who were called into our movement.

The Body of Christ

As well as reflecting something of the nature of God, our ministry should demonstrate the character of the Church as the Body of Christ. Where the New Testament speaks of the Body of Christ, it displays a picture of ministry in which all members contribute to the life of the Church through the exercise of gifts. No one is excluded because a contribution may be perceived to be small. The head of the Body is Christ himself. Its leaders exercise their ministry under his direction and in cooperation with all the Body's members (Ephesians 4:15, 16).

So there is a sense in which the whole congregation or Salvation Army corps is one ministry team, for: 'From him the whole body, joined and held together by every supporting ligament, grows and builds itself up in love, as each part does its work' (verse 16). Leaders, therefore, emerge from the Body. They are called by the Holy Spirit and are affirmed and appointed by the corps and its officers. They form themselves into a similar working unit, holding and supporting one another, growing in love and working together according to their various gifts.

Jürgen Moltmann, in his book, *The Church in the Power of the Spirit*, contends similarly that the work of the Church, its mission to declare and live out the gospel, rests in the hands of the whole people of God, not its ministers. This leads him to offer a model of leadership, where leaders emerge according to the particular mission task being undertaken:

> *It is clear that in determining the particular callings in a community we have to proceed from the calling of the community as a whole. The various ministries in the Church have the Church's single and common ministry as their presupposition and basis. The various forms of service presuppose the general service of the Kingdom of God, to which every believer belongs. The various assignments in the community, which can be distinguished from one another, are related to the common charge through Christ, the charge that reaches everyone (page 300).*

On the Church's commissioned leaders, Moltmann goes on to say:

> *How, then, are we to understand the position of these people, with their particular charges or assignments?*

They come from God's people, stand up in front of God's people and act in God's name. Their commission does not separate them from the people and does not set them above the people either, for it is exercised in fellowship with and by commission of the whole people and in the name of the people's commissioning. But the thing for which the people are commissioned does not come from themselves; it comes from their God, in whose name they speak and act (page 303).

Moltmann makes it clear that in presenting his model for team ministry he is not recommending any particular form of Church leadership over another. Church order is historical and relates to the underlying ethos on which the Church is built. For him, whatever the form of leadership may be, it must incorporate this understanding, that the mission is given to the whole people, and individuals are delegated to lead according to the abilities given to them in the power of the Spirit. Therefore, in the Army, we will retain our military form of government, as officers and soldiers take their places in ministry as the Spirit directs, but we will also be careful that our structures do not get in the way of the Army's mission in and to the modern world.

Mutual recognition of gifts

In order for consultative ministry to operate effectively within The Salvation Army, then, there needs to be first of all a mutual recognition of gifts. It is increasingly evident that, in a corps setting, the officer leader, no matter how gifted, cannot be expected to shoulder the multitude of responsibilities required today. He or she cannot be preacher and pastor, teacher and administrator, counsellor and hospital visitor to any but the smallest congregation. If the church is to grow, responsibility must be shared and the gifts of all recognised and used. It is not only important that people recognise their own gifts, but also that they are acknowledged and affirmed by the whole Body of Christ. This is especially important in the relationship between officers and soldiers and between officers and full-time employees of the Army. Good communication can lead to growth in trust and understanding and a much more creative use of all available gifts.

Alongside this, there is an urgent need for training, both for officers and for soldiers. Some officers still come from a background which has encouraged an individualistic style of leadership. Others recognise the importance of a shared vision and ownership, but find it difficult to develop a leadership style that grows and implements it.

Supportive line management, good mentoring and effective training will all help officers to develop the relevant skills. Soldiers, too, can benefit from training opportunities to develop new skills and to discover imaginative ways to put their commitment to, and passion for, the Army's vision into practice.

This kind of leadership is shared rather than individualistic. The Salvation Army, like all churches, desperately needs visionary leadership. Biblical and Church history reminds us of the inspiration of the founding leaders – of the nation of Israel, of the New Testament Church, of the Church universal, but the individual leader is also the servant of all, who puts the mission of the whole before personal ambition.

Consultative ministry focuses on the task rather than on the position of responsible individuals. The Church's task is to proclaim the gospel under the direction of God the Holy Spirit. It is vital to use those who have the right gifts for a particular enterprise. The mission-oriented church focuses on the task in hand and seeks out those best able to fulfil it for the sake of the Kingdom.

John R. W. Stott has been for more than 50 years part of the leadership team at All Souls Church in London. In an article entitled 'What Makes Leadership Christian?', published in *Christianity Today*, he suggests three reasons for the importance of consultative ministry. First, the members supplement one another, building on one another's strengths and compensating for one another's weaknesses. No leader has all the gifts, so no leader should keep all the reins of leadership in his or her hands. Second, the members encourage one another, identifying each of their gifts and motivating each other to develop and use them. Third, the members are accountable to one another. Shared work means shared responsibility. Members listen to one another and learn from one another. Both the human family and the divine family (the Body of Christ) are contexts of solidarity in which any incipient illusions of grandeur are rapidly dispelled. 'The way of a fool seems right to him, but a wise man listens to advice' (Proverbs 12:15).

A challenging opportunity

There are many ways in which officers and soldiers are already working together in what are effectively variations of team/consultative ministries. Young peoples' work and women's ministries are usually conducted on a team model, with groups of leaders planning a programme and taking varied responsibility for its operation. Corps council meetings and mission clusters, when they are properly understood and put into practice, provide excellent examples of team working.

However, team working is time-consuming and difficult, often chaotic and bewildering. It is a way of working that many approach with trepidation. To attempt to achieve goals by working according to different peoples' gifts is not necessarily a well-ordered process. It can be unstructured, messy and untidy. People are different, their gifts vary, they approach tasks – including the task of Christian ministry – very differently. Individuals may experience a loss of control as they work in the dark with no real idea of the final outcome of their service. To work separately according to one's own agenda, to retain some control over one's own part of the plan, can seem so much more straightforward.

What appears to be chaotic at times may be the most effective and creative way of exercising a Christian ministry. Consultative ministry is a constructive way of leadership to incorporate into the hierarchical structures on which our movement has been built. Prayerful reflection on this process may well enable us better to implement God's purposes for us as we move forward in our mission.

* * *

For group discussion

1. What does the phrase 'consultative ministry' mean to you?

2. Do you think such ministry is the most effective way to lead God's Army today?

3. Suggest a mission task your corps/centre is engaged in which would benefit from consultative leadership.

SECTION FOUR

THE LEADERSHIP OF GOD'S PEOPLE – ITS CHARACTER

Introduction

IN Romans 12:8, the apostle Paul says that if a person's gift is leadership he or she should govern diligently. The Greek term translated as leadership in this verse means 'ruling' and 'caring for'. Those two senses come together in 1 Timothy 3:12 where the same term is translated 'manage' in its application to the way in which the ideal deacon manages his children and his household well.

Closely associated with those who have the gift of leadership are those referred to in 1 Corinthians 12:28 as having .gifts of administration.. The Greek term for administration in this passage signifies 'steering'. It is also the term used for the pilot of a ship, as in Acts 27:11, the one in charge of getting a ship to its destination. It carries the sense of 'navigation' from one position to another.

Peter Wagner, in his book *Your Spiritual Gifts Can Help Your Church Grow*, makes a distinction between the gift of leadership on the one hand and administration on the other. He says that the gift of leadership has to do with setting goals in accordance with God's purpose for the future, and communicating those goals to others in such a way that they voluntarily and harmoniously work together to accomplish such goals for the glory of God. He distinguishes that gift from the gift of administration, which has to do with devising and executing effective plans for the accomplishment of goals.

In using the ship analogy, Wagner suggests that the administrator is like a helmsman who looks after the details of getting a ship to its destination, while the pastor/leader is like a ship's owner whose major role is that of a visionary who chooses the destination and then leaves it with others to get the ship there.

The two Greek terms translated as leadership and administration might also, however, be taken together in order fully to understand necessary components of leadership in general. The combined concept may be particularly helpful for an understanding of what it means to be servant leaders in the Christian Church.

Using a similar analogy to that of Peter Wagner, spiritual/ servant leaders are those who pilot the Church towards destinations determined through the guidance of God the Holy Spirit, the one who is ultimately the owner and inspires leaders with vision. Such leaders must be sensitive to spiritual direction in order to be aware of God's vision and God's ways of implementing that vision. Under God's guidance, they also have responsibility for caring for and motivating other members to work alongside them in seeing that the destination directed by God the Holy Spirit is reached. In other words, God calls and commissions certain members of the Body of Christ to be spiritual/servant leaders who work with others of the Body of Christ in setting Holy Spirit-directed goals, and in accomplishing those goals for the glory of God.

Prophets, priests and kings of the Old Testament were seen as spiritual/servant leaders involved in visioning, motivating and implementing. The ideal was fully seen and fulfilled in Jesus Christ. He became the leadership model for those whom he chose as his disciples and apostles. He is still the model for those he calls today to be leaders in the Church as his Body on earth.

Chapter Ten

PRIESTLY AND PROPHETIC ROLES

WE are concerned in these chapters with the character of leadership within The Salvation Army. What kind of leaders are we looking for, especially as the growth of the Church is to a large extent dependent upon the quality of its leaders? Some look for people to represent and serve their congregation – to speak 'for' the Christian community. They long for officers who can bring worship to life, make sense of the institutional aspects of our life together and can offer a personal model of true Christian discipleship. Others look for a more prophetic word.

They want leaders who can speak 'to' the movement, questioning its basic assumptions, challenging complacency and revealing the will of God in new, disturbing ways. Sometimes these characteristics are found in one leader. More often, leaders are gifted either as 'priests' or as 'prophets'. The Church – the Army – needs both.

Difficulties arise when one mode of leadership comes into conflict with the other. Sometimes the prophetic challenge stirs people up against the regular ministry and its organised life. Occasionally the organised ministry, which no longer meets the needs of the worshipping community, fails to open its heart to the prophetic word. Then sin bites into the heart of the Army's life and causes dissension.

We should not imagine that these problems are common to Salvationists only. Throughout the history of the Church, there has been the potential for conflict between priest and prophet.

The Old Testament

The Old Testament identified three kinds of recognised spiritual leaders among the Jews: priests, prophets and political leaders, or kings. The priests had two basic functions. The first was the maintenance of the spiritual and religious institutions of Israel, including especially the offering of religious sacrifices. The second was mediatory: to represent the people to God. The prophets, on the other hand, were not a formal religious order, though there were certain 'schools of prophets'.

One did not become a prophet because of a specific religious function, or by virtue of one's family of origin or one's formal training, but by special calling. Amos, for example, points out that he had none of the advantages of special birth or formalised training, but was only a herdsman and a tender of sycamore trees (Amos 7:14-15). On the other hand, the same person could be both a priest and a prophet, as in the case of Isaiah.

The function performed by the prophet was to represent God to the people. He was called to speak the mind and reveal the heart of God, exposing realities known only through divine revelation. He was to call to remembrance God's covenant with his people and its implications, to see and interpret God's future and to communicate both the mercy and the judgment of God. Performing this function was often risky, since it might call into question the religious life and practice of the community. It was not unusual for prophets to be ill-treated because of their insistence on delivering the Word of the Lord. It was a cost that they accepted sacrificially.

In the Old Testament we see conflict between priest and prophet appearing again and again, one representing the religious institution and the other the charisma that cannot be institutionalised. (See, for example, Amos 5:21-27; Isaiah 58.) The priest, by definition, was identified with the religious institution and its functions, and his role required institutional sanction. This identification undoubtedly predisposed him to a lack of objectivity about how religious practice and ritual may become substitutes for true righteousness and may even serve to assuage or protect worshippers from the guilt of their real disobedience. The prophet, by definition, did not require institutional identification and sanction and was, therefore, more predisposed to call the institution of religion and government into account or to judgment. We see here the seed of the tension in roles and functions between priest and prophet that continues to the present time.

The third group of spiritual leaders in the Old Testament was that of the political leaders or kings. In the Old Testament theocracy, the king was expected to take responsibility for spiritual leadership, as well as the social and economic welfare of the people. He was expected to lead his people in the paths of righteousness and was held accountable when he led them into apostasy. He was expected to use the considerable power with which he was invested to ensure the spiritual life of the nation and to maintain justice, especially for the poor and oppressed. The same was true for all persons who held political office and had power by virtue of their considerable wealth and position, including the priests, and, on occasions, the prophets.

Ezekiel 34 is a scathing indictment of those who have misused the power of their positions for self-aggrandisement and oppression and have abdicated their spiritual responsibilities.

New Testament teaching

In the New Testament, Jesus himself is the definitive model of spiritual leadership. His own ministry can be understood as a tripartite one of prophet, priest and king. Those who witnessed his coming, such as Simeon, saw him as the fulfilment of the hope that many in the Jewish religious institution had kept alive and nurtured over the years (Luke 2:25-32). They believed he would lead the nation back to its roots by restoring the purity of Israel's worship and mission. Yet, when his ministry began, he assumed rather the role of prophet. He stood outside the religious structures and unleashed floods of criticism against them and, like many of the prophets, he was treated cruelly for his message. Alongside his message of judgment was his message of hope. The prophetic ministry is always founded on hope; the prophet's critique is an invitation to clear away the obstructions to God's new future.

The priestly and prophetic roles of Jesus came together in the act of atonement. In his obedience to the will of God and his willingness to accept the Cross, Jesus followed perfectly the way of the prophets who had gone before him. In offering up himself as the perfect atoning sacrifice for sin, he served as our perfect mediator, 'a priest for ever, in the order of Melchizedek' (Psalm 110:4; Hebrews 5-7). In a sense, Jesus superseded both the priestly and prophetic roles; he was more than priest or prophet: he 'was' the Word; he 'was' the sacrifice.

He was able to combine the priestly and prophetic callings in such a way that there was no contradiction between them. For this reason, he is especially our model for spiritual leadership. The effective spiritual leader must be both.

Not only is Jesus regarded as priest and prophet, he is also king. During his life on earth, he rejected any claims to political leadership, but he exercised undoubted spiritual authority and claimed a spiritual Kingdom that his followers later understood and acknowledged. By his death, he won the battle against the forces of sin and darkness, so delivering us all from the powers that enslave us, and ushering in the Kingdom of God. And yet it was through obedience and servanthood that the victory was won. His model of leadership and authority subverted the prevailing ideas and set a model for a new kind of spiritual leadership. He saw himself as a servant leader.

In the history of the Church

Medieval Catholicism established a priesthood similar to the Old Testament model. The priest became part of a separated clergy, whose primary function was to offer the sacrifice of the Mass.

Prophets, in the sense of those who challenged the Church as an institution, were often regarded as heretics. Preaching was frequently undervalued.

The reformers rejected the medieval Catholic concept of priesthood, especially the central place given to the administration of the sacraments. They raised the profile of the proclaimed Word, and taught that the Church had not one, but two main functions, the preaching of the Word as well as the administration of the two sacraments of baptism and the Lord's Supper. Luther's dictum famously states: 'Where the Word of God is rightly preached and the sacraments rightly administered, there the true Church of God exists.'

Thus, in reformation theology, the Christian minister was both a preacher and the administrator of the sacrament. Worship that centred around the priest and the altar was replaced with worship that centred around the open Bible and the pulpit, with the preacher facing the congregation. The sacraments, too, were visible words of God. They proclaimed the forgiveness of sins and confirmed God's promises. So important was this function of proclamation that, while for both Martin Luther and John Calvin this ministry was the responsibility of the whole Church, in practice it should normally only be exercised by the one called to it and made accountable by the whole congregation. In effect, the ministry of Word and Sacrament came together in one person, the Christian minister.

Calvin elevated the role of the Christian minister – or pastor – almost to a model of the spiritual authority of Christ himself. Not only was the pastor the preacher, who distributed the Word of God to the congregation, he was also the ruler or governor of the Church, under the authority of Christ. His leadership and lifestyle were to be beyond reproach. 'Because [Christ] does not dwell among us in visible presence, he uses the ministry of men to declare openly his will to us by mouth, as a sort of delegated work' (*Institutes*, 4.3.1).

So, for the reformers, the whole Church was both priest and prophet. Through the sacraments, the congregation received the priestly ministry of the grace of God, as they offered that grace to one another in prayer and intercession. By hearing the Word of God preached in public week after week the Church proclaimed the gospel and was itself challenged to a life of purity and holiness. While the minister was the person effectively made accountable for these ministries, both the priestly and the prophetic roles were the responsibility of the whole people of God.

In The Salvation Army

This reformation understanding of universal responsibility and delegated authority is still very persuasive and is an important aid to our understanding of spiritual leadership in The Salvation Army. It is essential that the dual roles of priest and prophet are held within the ministry of the whole people of God. We are called to be a prophetic people, bearing witness to God's new life in Christ and challenging evil in Christ's name, both in our own movement and in the world around us. Sharing the good news in mission, teaching and learning, and managing the Church are the tasks of the whole Body of Christ.

We are also called to be a priestly people, receiving God's gift of grace and sharing it with one another and with the world in sacrificial service. If any one of these roles is largely delegated to officers, that must not mean that soldiers abdicate their responsibility. Nor should officers abdicate their responsibility for one role at the expense of the other. We are united in ministry, within the model of servant leadership that Jesus himself provides.

Salvation Army officers, and other leaders, are called to exercise both priestly and prophetic functions on behalf of the people of God.

They must nurture the spiritual life of the Army and also call into question any Salvationist practice that weakens its spirituality. They must maintain programme and service and also ensure that these are fulfilling the Army's mission. We need priests to maintain our religious practice, and we need prophets to call our religious practice into question. We need priests to intercede with God for the needs of the world, and we need prophets to challenge us to costly proclamation to that needy world. Without the former, we cannot cultivate our spiritual life; without the latter we cannot cultivate our spiritual integrity.

Sometimes officers are caught in the tension between these functions. As priests they maintain the Army, as prophets they call it into question. There are dangers in this tension. They may become so adept at speaking 'for' the institution that they lose the capacity to speak 'to' it. They may be tempted to individualise their prophetic role, challenging individuals, but failing to speak prophetically to the community as a whole. They will thus privatise prophecy. The priest-prophet tension is still with us. Understanding that this is so, and using the tension creatively and with compassion, is an important aspect of our developing theology of Christian ministry.

* * *

For group discussion

1. Discuss the place of prophecy in the Army today. Do you think this is a ministry we are in danger of neglecting?

2. Why is it important for the people of God to maintain the religious practices of the Church? What religious practices are vital for Salvationists to nurture and develop?

3. Is the tension that sometimes occurs within the Army due to priestly and prophetic roles a creative one?

Chapter Eleven
TRUE LEADERSHIP

GOD calls leaders in the Church to be models for all authentic leadership. Leadership within the Church has its special characteristics. It is overtly aligned with the mission of God in the world; it explicitly seeks to advance the cause of Christ; it is specifically aimed at mobilising a community of Christian faith to nurture the Kingdom of God in their own lives (holiness) and to seek its growth in the world (evangelism, caring service, social action). Just as the Church is called to be God's demonstration of community in the world, a model of the fulfilling life to which God calls all people, so God's Church leaders are called to demonstrate the kind of leadership to which he calls all leaders – a leadership of integrity and love.

The true leadership of which we are speaking is spiritual leadership, whatever the vocational or voluntary setting in which that leadership is exercised. Any other kind of leadership is a perversion – sometimes even an inversion – of true leadership, whether it is exercised inside or outside the Church. Church leaders are as fully tempted to false leadership as are 'secular' leaders. In fact, the subtlety of the temptation makes it insidiously powerful.

Who are the true leaders? They are not those who have achieved leadership perfection. We have all been taught or have caught leadership from imperfect models and texts. Our own sin has imbedded behaviour patterns which violate true leadership and which are replaced only through prayer, good mentoring and strong self-discipline. True leadership is a lifelong pursuit requiring humble self-acceptance, intense personal honesty, confession of shortcomings and sin, a guiding vision to advance the Kingdom of God, a deep care for others and, above all, love for God and desire to please him above all others. True leaders are those who are on a determined journey. They never claim to have arrived. They are always becoming leaders.

How do they nurture their leadership? How do they measure their progress? This chapter will consider 10 key characteristics of true leadership. These are characteristics of true leadership in any setting. They are the characteristics in particular which Church leaders are called to model for all leaders, the characteristics which make all leaders effective in terms of the only measurement of real value: the Kingdom of God. Other measurements settle for less or look for the wrong things, but these measurements profile a leadership that grows the enduring Kingdom and guides people to it. They are the qualities that are nurtured by true leaders in themselves and in others.

1. Calling

True leadership is 'called' leadership. Within each vocation each person is called to demonstrate the true purpose of that vocation, to be a model of how that purpose is realised, to lead by example. In the Church, likewise, leaders are called to 'be shepherds of God's flock ... not lording it over those entrusted to you, but being examples to the flock' (1 Peter 5:2, 3). Leadership has nothing to do with gaining advantage, leveraging position, accumulating power, building empires or manipulating weak or beholden followers – even when these ends are pursued by apparently moral people. It has to do with contributing to people's lives, sharing power, nurturing leadership in others, building community, helping others to release their creativity, pursuing a vision of God's future for the world. It is how we follow a calling, not how we build a career.

In a world driven by the obsession to win at all costs, the concept of a calling is countercultural. For the Christian, the concepts of calling and career occupy opposite ends of the spectrum of life work. Calling implies pursuit of a God-given vision, a task within that vision and a community to share fully in it. Career implies pursuit of a self-serving agenda, upward mobility towards greater advantages and beating the competition. The two are basically irreconcilable. The called leader faces the enormous challenge to free himself or herself, the Church and the world from the obsession with winning.

Christian leaders ideally are those who practise and model this calling. They summon the world to dream God's dream, to live transformed lives and to share in Christ's mission. They keep the larger vision the dominant force in their work. God's inclusive vision of the world's salvation is what drives them. Their gifts are developed and deployed unselfishly for God and for the world which he loves and redeems (John 3:16). This is the true leadership which Christian leaders are called to teach to the world.

All true leadership, therefore, is leadership under divine orders. A higher allegiance continually illumines and refines personal motives; a higher accountability establishes eternal priorities. All other allegiances and forums of accountability are relative in importance to this.

How is such a calling possible, especially in a world that conditions people to place their personal interests first? The answer lies in the second quality of true leadership.

2. Spiritual depth

The strength of character, the courage, the breadth of compassion and the vision commitment of true leaders require familiarity with the divine. It is the presence of God in leaders' lives that keeps them true to their calling. Like David, leader of Israel, they know that the heavy demands of their calling must not keep them from their worship, their adoration of God and their reflection in his presence (Psalm 27:4). This is quite different from an affected godliness, a facade of public piety to gain easy credibility. It is the fruit of a strong relationship with God cultivated through the discipline of prayer, encounter with God's Word, meditation and self-denial. God's way is not ours; it can only be travelled, taught and modelled by those who go to great lengths to know God.

As 'stewards of the mysteries of God' (1 Corinthians 4:1, *RSV*), Christian leaders have an understanding and carry a compassion that comes from the mind and heart of God himself. Acquainted with God, they become more like him (Ephesians 5:1). As this relationship is strengthened, so is their awareness of the spiritual authority of their leadership. Less and less do they rely upon the institutional authority invested in their office or the popular authority given because of their natural talents or personal charm. More and more do they rely upon the authority of holiness, the manifestation of the divine in their lives, the transformation of their heart and the renewal of their mind, and the blessing, encouragement and confirmation of God.

Since leadership is a calling, the leader must know the caller and discern the call. In this sense, surprisingly, leaders are like sheep that know the shepherd's voice and respond to his guidance and care (John 10:14-16). They trust the voice. Inevitably, the voice asks them to brave the unknown or take the road less travelled. This is what true leaders are called to do, because they are sheep who obey the extraordinary call of Christ their Shepherd by acts of unselfishness, compassion and courage.

3. Courage

True leadership requires courage. The Bible and Church history show models of courage that were often extraordinary. Church leaders today are called to no less a strength of character. When they model timid leadership, however, others are influenced towards cowardice. Christian living becomes compromised, calling becomes vague, risk-taking becomes too costly and Christ's mission is reduced to social acceptability. True leadership is always marked by courage.

Let us be clear where this courage originates. The courage of which we speak is not a natural personality trait. Some people are more courageous by nature, but we are speaking of the extraordinary courage of those from whom we may least expect it. This courage does not come from personality but from spiritual depth and from answering a call. It is something given when God calls a leader to do the unexpected thing, to go against the safe course, to break new ground and to risk failure.

It is the gift given to Gideon when God calls him to leadership. Gideon understandably objects. "'But Lord,' Gideon asked, "how can I save Israel? My clan is the weakest in Manasseh, and I am the least in my family"' (Judges 6:15). And God promises, 'I will be with you' (6:16). It is the gift given to the prophet Amos, a common herdsman, who, without any institutional backing whatsoever, stands alone against the political and religious power structures with only a divine call and presence to steady him. It is the gift given to the apostle Paul, who braves beatings, assassination attempts, hostile religious councils and powerful governors because Christ is all that finally matters to him, and his apostolic call is his magnificent obsession. It is the gift given to William and Catherine Booth and the early Salvationists who braved both physical attack on the streets and ridicule in the secular and religious press to shape their movement and methods to follow a call to the poor of London and then the world. It is no accident that the call and the courage emerged from the spiritual depths of a holiness people.

Leaders are called to be models of such courage. In this they encourage others. The secret of such courage, the source of such strength, is an ongoing communion with God, an abandonment to him and a surrender to his calling – none of which is possible without personal discipline.

4. Personal discipline

There is a misconception that highly courageous people are usually not self-disciplined. This would be true of reckless people, but not the truly courageous. Courage is the fruit not only of God's supportive presence and clear call, but also of a disciplined life. The courage of true leaders is forged by the life focus and strong purpose of those who discipline themselves to major on the essentials and painstakingly discern God's leading. The apostle Paul assures young Timothy that the Spirit's gift is power, love and self-discipline, not timidity (2 Timothy 1:7). What is interesting about this statement is that it not only links self-discipline with courage but it also speaks of self-discipline as a gift, something the Spirit gives. In an earlier letter to Timothy, Paul points out how crucial it is to claim and exercise the gift of self-discipline: 'Do not neglect your gift, which was given you through a prophetic message when the body of elders laid their hands on you. Be diligent in these matters; give yourself wholly to them, so that everyone may see your progress. Watch your life and doctrine closely. Persevere in them, because if you do, you will save both yourself and your hearers' (1 Timothy 4:14-16).

This attentiveness to one's life and thought is, for Paul, a life-and-death matter. Without self-discipline our lives will wander at will and we will find ourselves absorbed in lesser pursuits and even idolatrous behaviour. Our leadership will also suffer seriously, as we will lose clarity about how we can work out our calling, and our strong sense of direction will give way to a short-sighted absorption in smaller things. Self-discipline is both the planned daily reminder of our calling and the sustained effort that enables us to discern and develop that calling.

Notice that Paul mentions not only ourselves, but also our 'hearers'. Our lack of self-discipline will affect others. Those who look to us and work with us will have less and less confidence in where we are going and what we are about. Undisciplined church leaders are a poor – indeed, a damaging – model of leadership. They teach others that a purposeful calling can be compromised.

True leadership that advances Christ's mission is characterised by personal discipline. All true leaders use this gift. It keeps them focused on what is of ultimate importance in their life's work. It also keeps them focused on 'who' is of ultimate importance. We discipline ourselves not to become absorbed in our personal agendas but to become more sensitive to the presence and value of others.

5. Relationship-building

In a world of personal disconnection and social alienation, the search for relationships and community is stronger than ever. In fact, it is often desperate, so desperate that people settle for superficial personal connections and unhealthy affiliations just to be in some kind of relationship and to participate in some form of community. As God's vision for his fallen world is a vision of restored community and shared love, so true leadership models the relationship-building of those who have claimed that vision.

True leaders care about relationships and build community. This does not mean that they must be extroverts, nor that they have a deep need to be with people most of the time. What is decisive for leadership is the caring, the healing of relationships and the strengthening of true community.

True leadership does not emerge in isolation. It emerges in the context of a community of faith, and it aims at nurturing that community towards the shared life of the Kingdom of God. The decisive model is Jesus, who built relationships and used his authority to authorise others. He formed a relational group called disciples and invited them to love one another (John 13:34). He launched a relational project called mission and invited the world to discover the love of God (John 3:16) and of neighbour (Mark 12:31). Wherever he went, he made connections and drew people into his circle, even those considered the worst sinners (for example, the adulterous woman in John 8:2-11). Jesus is the needed leadership model for a polarised society.

Relationship-building then extends beyond the leader's immediate community. Leaders who are concerned almost exclusively with their own immediate group – whether that group is a family, a church, or some other social or economic unit – are leaders with a misguided understanding of leadership. They fail to see that the more exclusive and limiting the relational concern, the more unhealthy the relationships. A family focused on itself becomes smothering; a church preoccupied with its own life loses its mission. In a networking world, Christian leaders have almost unlimited capacity to build, strengthen, deepen and redeem relationships through and for Christ. True leadership opens doors to the world.

Nowhere is such a calling more powerfully profiled than in the Church, where members worship one who loved the whole world and died for it. Jesus died not only for the Jewish nation, but also 'for the scattered children of God, to bring them together and make them one' (John 11:52). In Matthew's Gospel, Jesus gives a final, parting command to his disciples: 'Go and make disciples of all nations' (Matthew 28:19). As followers of Christ, Church leaders are called to be models of an inclusive relationship-building which encompasses all nations and cultures. This quality is best expressed and this mission made most effective when a leader demonstrates servanthood.

6. Servanthood

A servant leader is one who sits at the feet, and travels in the company of the one who said, 'whoever wants to become great among you must be your servant' (Mark 10:43). When leadership is seen as the ability to use power to get one's way, the concept of 'servant leadership' is a contradiction in terms. From a biblical perspective, however, it is a perfect fit. Jesus, of course, is the model.

Think of the foot washing (John 13:1-17), of his voluntarily taking the form of a servant (literally, 'slave'), of his declaration that, 'If anyone wants to be first, he must be the very last, and the servant of all' (Mark 9:35). Jesus said of himself, 'I am among you as one who serves' (Luke 22:27).

Servant leadership is not weak leadership. It is the most powerful of all. Servant leaders discover power by giving it up. They refuse to use their positions to control people or to use them as stepping stones. They enhance power by sharing it with others. Like Jesus, they use their authority to authorise others. The power of servanthood is the only power that builds an enduring Kingdom. It really is the meek who will inherit the earth (Matthew 5:5).

Servanthood is the mission of the Church. It is the calling that pervades all callings. It is not true that some leaders are called to be servants while others are not. All callings are exercised by servants, or they are degraded. Prophets who are not servants become arrogant and thus their message is easily dismissed. Priests who are not servants become obsessed with their positions and thus their ministry is only self-service. Pastors who are not servants become manipulative and thus their help is not helpful. The calling to servanthood is decisive for the realisation of all callings.

Inside and outside the Church, the ever-present temptation for leaders is power intoxication. To avoid this, they must take their authority seriously and exercise their power responsibly, but they must not be captivated by it. They understand that the power entrusted to them is the power to empower others.

7. Empowerment of others

The New Testament is clear that the Son of the all-powerful God never used his power to his own advantage but 'made himself nothing, taking the very nature of a servant!' (Philippians 2:7). The outcome of this self-emptying was revolutionary because it was used to empower others. Incredible power was released to those who believed in his name, power to become children of God and heirs to the Kingdom (John 1:12-13; Galatians 4:1-7). Weak disciples were promised Pentecostal power – power not to fashion an ecclesiastical empire but power to witness (Acts 1:8). True leaders empower others for the freedom of servanthood, not for the slavery of self-promotion.

How does this empowerment take place in the Church? It takes place primarily through 'mentoring' and 'discipling'. True Christian leaders invest themselves in guiding, training and teaching others. They do this to empower them to become disciples of Jesus Christ, not to become disciples of themselves. They do it to empower them to become strong Christian leaders serving Christ.

As leaders develop, they learn to delegate. Delegation is the sharing of power and responsibility with appropriately gifted persons. As these persons respond to this trust, they grow into leadership and, in turn, learn to empower others. True leaders give away power. This donation of power to others releases leaders from desperate grasping and frees their heart and mind and action for creativity.

8. Creativity

The exercise of creativity is a potent expression of who we are: creatures made in the image of God. God is creator, and when we create we are mirroring him and thereby affirming our humanity. We are discovering our freedom in Christ. The Church is called to be a place where this freedom is nurtured.

True leadership is not wedded to unchanging policies and procedures. The Church's mission requires a willingness to see totally new possibilities and move beyond ingrained habit. The same is true of the mission of any person or group that intends to impact the world significantly. Creativity is a mark of leadership.

Leadership is sometimes confused with management. A manager deals with the given; he/she keeps things intact and running smoothly and efficiently. Management is not opposed to leadership so long as it does not attempt to smother creativity. And leadership cannot do without the management that prevents complete chaos and maintains a needed level of order.

Good managers always have a flash of creative leadership. If they focus entirely on internal process and efficiency and ignore a changing landscape, whatever they are managing will become increasingly irrelevant and useless. But if they read the signs of the times, think creatively about adaptation of methods and measures and risk change, they will be effective. If they do no more than manage, they will not be good managers.

There are many functions within the Body of Christ. Some functions require greater emphasis upon management and maintenance, others on visioning and creativity. What is crucial is that everyone be encouraged to dream and to be creative in his or her ministries. This will happen when the focus is on the Church's mission in an ever-changing terrain. It will happen when there is passion for mission.

9. Passion for mission

The mission field is the test of the Church's real effectiveness, and therefore of its leadership. If the mission of Christ is not succeeding, leadership is failing. For this reason, true leadership is passionate for mission. Leadership's passion must be focused on the world for whom Christ died – the suffering, fragmented world. The world, as Wesley said, must be our parish.

Passion for mission, however, does not require ignoring the needs of the congregation, failing to disciple the faithful, or giving no attention to stewardship and order in the church. It requires carrying out these ministries with an eye always on mission. As the members of the fellowship receive and give pastoral care, they are taught to care for the world and, by that, to demonstrate to the world the power of love. As they are discipled, they are equipped to let their lights shine in the world, prepared for the ministries for which they are gifted and sent out as missionaries. They are encouraged to order their lives in the world and condition themselves for mission.

Focus on mission also makes successful leadership development at the local level an absolute necessity. Leadership training for both officers and soldiers must focus on training persons for leadership in both corps and communities. If a leader is distracted from mission in any way, true leadership will be abandoned. Conversely, if there is passion for mission, true leadership will be found.

10. Personal and vocational growth

All the qualities we have discussed require a final component of the leadership profile. These qualities do not develop on their own, especially in a world that does not encourage them. They are the fruit of experience guided by a discipline of personal and vocational growth. True leaders evaluate themselves, set goals for their own development and accomplish them. They also draw upon the wisdom and consultation of mentors and coaches.

The process of self-evaluation will nurture tomorrow's leaders. True leadership is not possible without planned growth both in one's personal life and in one's vocation, and the beginning point of such growth is honest, perceptive self-assessment. The growth plan must be founded on reality. The leader's self assessment can draw upon the apostle Paul's admonition to think of ourselves 'with sober judgment' (Romans 12:3). For some, the admonition invites a greater modesty, for others a greater self-appreciation, for all an examined life. True leaders know themselves, their strengths, their temptations, and their progress.

They also know a way forward in their development. This knowledge comes from where they are on their own spiritual journey, the direction of their calling, the identification of their God-given gifts and needed skill development, the ministry in which they

are involved (or plan to be involved) and self-assessment. Self-assessment comes from answers to key questions:
- Where am I on my spiritual journey and in what ways do I want to draw nearer to God and know him (and therefore myself) better?
- What is God specifically calling me to be and do?
- What are my gifts and how is God calling me to develop and use them?
- What particular skills would it be helpful for me to develop for greater effectiveness at the present time?

Answers to these questions are best shared in an accountability group or coaching team and refined in dialogue with such groups. Prayerfully considered and arrived at, they provide the first key component of the leader's development.

The second step in determining the way forward is the development of a personal and vocational growth plan. What is important is that the plan be both challenging (requiring the effort, discipline and discomfort that all true growth requires) and realistic (not so ambitious as to guarantee superficiality or failure).

An excellent growth plan will focus on what is truly important for one's spiritual and personal life and for one's calling and leadership effectiveness. Crucial components of such a plan should be:

- Cultivation of a leader's relationship with God.
- The preservation and nurturing of a leader's relational life (marriage, family, friends).
- Cultivating and utilising gifts.
- Emphasis on a leader's continuing education.

The third step is gaining the help of consultants and mentors. This help takes the form of coaching and resourcing. Moving forward in development is in the hands of the leaders themselves, but they share their self-evaluation and growth plan with their consultants and the consultants share their wisdom. When that wisdom has been shared, a final written document is decided by the leaders and this becomes the plan that is now implemented.

The final component in personal development is the monitoring of progress and the measurement of success. This final measurement is included in the self-evaluative process which launches the next phase. Usually, the plan runs by a yearly cycle; however, it is wise to think in the longer term – say, three years – so that the sequence of the plan makes good sense developmentally.

Whatever the specific format of the growth plan, what is essential for true leadership is a strategy for one's ongoing development spiritually, personally and vocationally. Leadership is strengthened by intentional nurture, as it is weakened by developmental neglect.

This profile of true leadership is presented as a guide to draw upon and consult. It is not intended as a 'rating card' for perfectionists. Whereas all true leaders will have each of the 10 qualities to some degree, they will be stronger and more intentional in some than in others. The purpose of the profile is to provide a template of leadership shaped by a Christian outlook and by the values of the Kingdom of God. Any of us can be this kind of leader, at least in some ways, no matter what our gifting and the extent of organisational authority that has been invested in us. The bare wielding of the power of an office, in and of itself, leaves no legacy of value. The influence of true leadership, whether or not connected with a substantial organisational position, is incalculable.

*　*　*

For group discussion

1. Have each group member come prepared to identify which one or two (no more!) of the qualities of true Christian leadership are important for his or her own personal development at this time, and to discuss why that quality is crucial now.

2. Discuss various resources that are available for developing the special leadership qualities described in this section.

3. Discuss the leadership qualities that you think are strongest in your corps. How can your corps build on those qualities? What other qualities do you think need to be developed further?

Chapter Twelve

THE FUTURE OF LEADERSHIP

WHAT will true leadership look like in the 21st century? What model will the Church offer as it responds to Christ's call to go and make disciples, nurture saints and serve compassionately? What shape will officership and all forms of spiritual leadership in The Salvation Army take?

We can be sure that God's people will continue to be called to worship, community and mission, however the features and forms may change. We can also be sure that in a world of growing complexity, Christian vocations will continue to diversify, specialisations will increase and the contribution of the giftings of all believers will be more essential than ever. Finally, we can be sure that true leadership – modelled in the ministry and mission of God's People – will be needed more than ever.

As human mobility increases and the mission field changes more rapidly, the commissioning of Christian leaders to a wide diversity of field-responsive callings will be crucial. In this broken world, the healing, restorative influence of servant leadership will bring reconciliation. As specialisations increase and knowledge expands, the leader will be most fruitful and influential in a team setting where each person's contribution is multiplied by the partnership and skills of others.

This chapter is devoted to profiling the leadership that is emerging as the whole people of God face the future into which God is leading them. In particular, it will draw from the biblical model of leadership those qualities and characteristics that have crucial relevance for that future. It will suggest a paradigm of spiritual leadership for the 21st century.

What will all this mean for The Salvation Army? We cannot be entirely sure, but there are some directions we most surely will be taking. For example, we know that the opportunities for full-time spiritual leadership will expand both within officership and alongside it. We know that officership will change its face, though not its heart. We know that for some the call to full-time Christian leadership will be less tied to lifelong officership in The Salvation Army, but instead may include periods of short-term service. We also know that, in some countries, we will see the traditional model of officers married only to officers altered for those married couples where spouses have separate callings that are incompatible within that model. Also we know that as cultural, social and ethnic diversity impact on our movement, stereotypical corps will be replaced by contrasting models, each requiring specific leadership gifts and training for accomplishing the same mission of God.

The crucial task of Army leadership is to turn the heart of people towards life in God. The Salvation Army has historically attracted and cultivated leaders who confronted destructive forces and led the way to restored life. Today, those forces may take different forms, but they still must be confronted. Some of them may also exist within our movement, pulling us away from our mission and from Kingdom-based living. Hence, our future as an effective Army of God rests with how successful we are in developing leaders who nurture our life with God, our life together and our life in the world.

This chapter will identify important challenges facing Christian leadership in the 21st century. The qualities of true leadership described in Chapter 11 will be further developed as responses to those challenges. Those responses will focus on conceptual, personal and organisational changes.

1. Calling in a world driven by competition

How do we conceive of the calling to leadership in a world that continues to be driven by competition? We see it as a calling to build community by respecting and nurturing the dignity of others. It is a calling that calls others to embrace their Christian vocations. It builds bridges between the Church and the common people. It rejects all élitisms, especially the clerical.

Christian leaders are called into the world to be icons – windows to God. Missional leadership is not a matter of style or methodology, it is a matter of helping people see God, hear his voice, experience his acceptance, receive his healing and be empowered for his future. It is a matter of guiding people into the family of God and full participation in the Kingdom of God. It is leadership as a calling, not a career. It follows Christ and invites the world to pilgrimage. It opens windows to God and doors to life.

Such leaders must make significant personal changes. In a competition-driven field, they will be compassion-driven. In an organisational environment which values positions of authority, they will exercise spiritual authority. As those who value their calling rather than a career, they will have a clear mission, one which is not tied to organisational success or even identification, but to people whose lives will be changed, to a compassionate community that will be cultivated.

What does all this mean for The Salvation Army of the future? It means:

1. Continuing strongly to define officership in terms of calling rather than career, and treating it as such. Vocational planning is important. While honouring the principle of the officer's availability, the veil of mystery or tight confidentiality that can sometimes surround the appointment process will need to be still further removed to allow for the easy and natural consultation that builds trust and confidence. Much progress in recent years been seen in this. It releases leaders to respond to God's continual call and so fulfil their vocation.

2. Measuring success primarily in terms of the purposes of the calling rather than in terms of other objectives. If calling has to do with contribution to the spiritual growth of a community, to the

development of mature disciples of Jesus, to substantive caring ministries, to serving the mission and the community of faith, then the first measure of success must be the leader's effectiveness in accomplishing these aspects of the calling. This means, of course, that, in the case of Army officers, terms of appointment must be of sufficient length to allow for substantive ministry to take root and spiritual leadership success to be measured. The appointment process must be used neither for organisational convenience (solving an immediate problem) nor for individual career advancement; it must be used to enhance the spiritual strength of the mission field.

3. The full deployment of the gifts of the Spirit and full recognition of the passions of the heart. As far as possible, leaders must be placed in appointments that match giftings and release the passions of their calling. In the case of officer couples, the appointment process must honour respective and mutual giftings; and in some instances, where the callings of each spouse are incompatible within the traditional model of married officership, consideration should be given to a more appropriate model involving an officer married to a non-officer. In the case of all officers, opportunity for the development of individual gifts for spiritual leadership and ministry is crucial, as well as the development of a shared ministry by many officer couples.

4. Affirming specialised callings more than ever and making short-term service more viable. As the calling of officers is increasingly seen to be independent of the specific organisation or a particular 'service path' within it, officership will take different forms. 'Tent-making', for example, is a possibility, where an officer supports his or her ministry through 'outside' employment.

2. Spiritual depth in a world of shallowness

The leaders of tomorrow will confront shallow spirituality. The world will not be without religious belief; it will be without spiritual depth. Religiosity will flood the market; but genuine faith will go looking for disciples. The incessant longing for ultimate answers will drive people to believe almost anything.

How will we frame leadership in a world where belief is easy and depth is difficult? We will frame it as a calling to exercise the spiritual disciplines as well as the gifts of the Spirit. The shallowness of contemporary spirituality needs the depth of spiritual truth and vitality. The word of truth, so often compromised and confused within the Church, must be discovered through disciplined study of the Word of God, teaching and preaching. Leaders must not only be people who are in touch with the world; they must be lifelong disciples of Christ.

Leadership in an age of religious pluralism must mediate the God of Jesus. In order to do so, the theological integrity and biblical training of leaders will be important. More essential will be their closeness to God and holiness of life. More essential will be leaders whose hearts are filled with God. More essential will be their depth.

Such leaders will allow God to change them and will place themselves where change can take place. They will place themselves within the consistent discipline of the Spirit and take advantage of opportunities for spiritual formation. They will choose spiritual mentors and guides, people with whom they meet and to whom they are accountable on a regular basis. In this way, they will take responsibility for their own spiritual development and for constructing some means through which to practise that accountability. This will focus more on who they are than on what they do.

What are the implications of this understanding of leadership for the Army of the future?

First, it clearly means that spiritual depth must be the first and most important qualification for officership and all spiritual leadership. To be sure, spiritual leadership requires appropriate gifting and ongoing training, but the centre of it, without which this leadership cannot hold together, is the presence of God, the essential qualification and validation. When leaders stand before the people to lead worship or teach truth, when they sit among the people to counsel, or when they walk alongside the people to understand and guide, they do so first as men and women who have been with Jesus.

Second, this understanding of leadership requires not only that the Army provide resources for the spiritual development of its leaders, but that it also offers a means of accountability for spiritual progress and remedy for spiritual lapse. There must be an organisational discipline for training leaders in righteousness and guiding them in holiness. There must be ways to invite leaders to account for their relationship with God. There must be a support system for the weakened who need strength and the casualties who need healing. In a world of spiritual shallowness, where Christian leaders must bring depth, the Army must invest heavily in spiritual life development and support. Our teaching on the holy life, on the blessing of a clean heart, will be at the centre of all this.

3. Courage in a world of fear-driven caution

Love of God and of others is alone the source of true courage. Perfect love, and it alone, casts out fear (1 John 4:18).

The real spiritual leaders of the Church will continue to be those who allow the love of God to claim them and change them. They will be so taken by that love that it will drive them to take risks and put their lives on the line for it. By their example and encouragement they will invite fellow believers to be people of courage. Sometimes the courage will be prophetic: risking being ostracised for speaking the truth in love. Sometimes it will be priestly: suffering with those who suffer, or even in their stead. Sometimes it will be missional: expanding the boundaries of mission into new territory. Always it will be compassion-driven.

The Army will sometimes need to change in order to accommodate and even encourage such risk-taking. The tendency of institutionalised organisations is to engender caution and protect the organisation. Ironically, the best way to ensure the continued growth and vitality of the organisation is to nurture and reward the kinds of wise, mission-focused risks that originally made the organisation so strong and released such compassion.

The Army of the 21st century must not abandon its heritage of risk-taking. It must take strategic risks, as well as agree on strategic abandonments (for example, the closing of failed corps). It must be willing to experiment with new approaches when old ones have failed. If the Army continues to encourage and reward risk-taking for its mission, it will also continue to be a place where compassion thrives.

4. Personal discipline in a world without focus

The leadership of the future will be exercised in a world of many distractions. The leaders who will give clear direction amid this growing distraction are those who claim and exercise the gift of personal self-discipline. Self-discipline is the practice of setting priorities and living by them. It is making sure that first things get first place. It is giving up the lesser for the more important. It is a non-negotiable requirement for pursuing a calling.

In this century, Army leaders will model this self-discipline for others. They will do it in many ways. Here are some:

- ◆ They will follow the disciplines of the Spirit and carefully guard their time with God.
- ◆ They will set missional and ministry priorities and live by them.
- ◆ They will not allow themselves to be spread too thinly over too varied a range of responsibilities or to be pulled in too many directions.
- ◆ They will concentrate on developing their own spiritual gifts and key strengths so as to make the contribution they are uniquely called to make.

◆ They will also strengthen their weaker areas in order to exercise sufficient competence in those areas.

This kind of personal discipline will enable Army leaders to show how the Christian life is to be lived in a world distracted and without direction. Salvation Army administration and its processes must encourage this kind of personal discipline in its leaders. Without this support, disciplined leadership will be more difficult, and, for some, perhaps impossible. Here are some essential components of this support:

◆ Organisational procedures will be kept as lean and mission-directed as possible.
◆ Accountability will focus primarily on the things that are most important for the leader to accomplish.
◆ Accomplishments will be valued according to their significance for the Army's mission.
◆ Leaders will be helped to achieve sufficient knowledge and competence to manage resources and recruit people where necessary.

5. Relationship-building in an alienated world

Leadership in this century must not only bring focus and discipline, it must also build relationships. The world not only lacks direction, it lacks connection. Alienation and the loss of community are endemic, and, for many, the future seems to hold little hope for reconnection. We have not handled pluralism well; racial hatred continues; ethnic violence proliferates. Dialogue is rare and the language of polarisation is common. Perhaps the most challenging task of leadership will be to nurture compassion and connection.

How will our leaders address alienation? They will do the following:

- Leaders will build inclusive relationships of caring. They will nurture compassion and form groups where members connect with one another. They will be relational pastors who are able to share the joy and suffering of life with others.
- Leaders will build compassionate communities that are interconnected, united in diversity, friendly and open. They will lead worship that brings people into the presence of God and the fellowship of his universal family. They will facilitate reconciliation and consensus and unite people around common purposes.

How will Army administration encourage this relational leadership in its leaders? It will:

- Focus its leadership training on the development of caring shepherds and place effectiveness in this ministry as a very high criterion in leadership evaluation.
- Train leaders to develop their relational skills by schooling them in counselling and coaching.
- Affirm the ministry of leaders in all areas of Army life.

6. Servanthood in a world of self-centredness

Self-centredness is a pervasive mindset of civilisation, a formidable enemy of the values of God's family. It is the equivalent of the apostle Paul's term, the 'flesh', that presumptuous inclination of fallen human nature to seek self-fulfilment in the indulgence of the self, rather than the way of the Spirit. It is a mindset that has no conqueror other than genuine servanthood (Philippians 2:1-11), and that conquest is led by servant leaders who share and use power unselfishly.

What will this servant leadership mean for Army leadership in this century? It will mean:

- The exercise of spiritual gifts in humility, as a service to the Body of Christ and to the world.
- Leaders becoming those who model servanthood before the community.
- A selfless focus on using one's gifts in service, and not for personal advancement.
- The elevation of all callings to places of importance.
- Helping the world to see that servanthood is the key to all callings.

The Army will continue to nurture servanthood. The power of a servant is the only power that brings the Kingdom of God to life and frees people from slavery to self-interest.

7. Empowerment of others in a power-grasping world

In the 21st century, leadership will be exercised in a culture that honours power. People have been taught to grasp and hold, not to claim and give away. Whether the power accumulation is political, economic, social, relational or ecclesiastical, the two outcomes are the moral and spiritual corruption of those who cling to the power and the disempowerment of others

Both the power-graspers and the disempowered need liberation. It will come as those who have power share it and sometimes give it up, and as those who feel powerless come to realise the power they do have and exercise it. It will come as leaders discover the truth of Jesus' life: power is redemptive when it is given away in love.

True Christian leadership will follow the self-emptying Christ. It will learn to give power away responsibly but generously. It will discover that the influence of character and the force of example are far more powerful than the exercise of the power of a position.

To meet the challenge of a power-grasping world, the Army will need leaders who:

- Nurture communities of empowerment and enablement (corps, institutions and headquarters).
- Specifically empower those in our fellowships who in a particular culture have been disempowered (for example, ethnic minorities, and women).
- Mentor officers and other leaders in the art of sharing power without abdicating responsibility.
- Activate soldiers who are at present non-participating.

The Army will need also to continue to address and review creatively its own systems and processes in order for empowerment to take place. It will need to:

- Hold officers accountable for how well they increase their own effectiveness by empowering others.
- Train officers in the art of delegation.
- Provide training in how to empower corps.
- Give focused attention to empowering soldiers.
- Focus on appointing officers where their gifts can be effectively deployed.

8. Creativity in a world of conformity

Christian leadership must model a creative God who makes all things new and releases persons from the shackles of conformity. Christian leaders must be willing to dream differently and encourage others to do so. They must not allow conformity to block mission and smother the creativity of God's people.

While honouring our heritage and affirming the best in our traditions, Salvationist leaders will build creatively on them. They will claim the leadership models of our history that reveal our bold ingenuity and genius for improvisation. They will risk breaking the moulds of procedures that no longer serve our mission. As leaders of worship, they will be artists for God, venturing into new expressions of creative worship. As preachers, they will connect the Word of God with the realities of life in new ways. As administrators, they will be constantly looking for new ideas to renew the organisation and keep its processes in line with the Army's mission.

More specifically, the Army itself will need to go on taking significant steps to encourage creative leadership. Here are some of them:

- Affirm creative, even unorthodox thinkers and doers who open previously closed doors and create new possibilities.
- Encourage missional and organisational creativity by affirming quality failures. Leaders can be affirmed for taking bold steps to advance Christ's mission, and for testing a new idea for ministry. Strong affirmation for 'good failures' always encourages our missional entrepreneurs.
- Allow some flexibility in appointment and assignment designations.
- Avoid the temptation to gain acceptance in the wider ecclesiastical world by uncritically adopting practices, rituals and terminologies that devalue our own creative history.

9. Passion for mission in a rootless world

The mission field is a constantly shifting terrain and the rate of change will only increase in this century. Without missional ingenuity driven by a passion to reach people for Christ in a changing environment, mission will die for lack of sanctified imagination.

The passion to reach people for Christ leads to creativity in mission. In a world of change, contextualisation of the gospel is an ongoing process and mission is mobile.

Here the role of the spiritual leader in developing and empowering local leaders is crucial. Understanding the shifting terrain is impossible for one person. Local leaders must be trained to reach their individual plots of that terrain, the places they know and are known in. The spiritual leader must sustain and nurture local leaders, equipping them to minister in their respective places. Without this localisation of leadership, people on the ever-changing mission field will be lost to the Kingdom of God.

The Army in the new century must go on enlisting and developing passionate mission-focused spiritual leaders. Some of the key actions to assist this are:

- ♦ Make a concerted effort to recruit capable, gifted officer candidates who intend to pursue their calling in corps or centre appointments.
- ♦ In evaluating spiritual leaders, place mission-effectiveness above managerial efficiency.
- ♦ Give corps/centre leaders significant recognition for their accomplishments and affirm competent leaders who choose that location of their ministry for the duration of their service.
- ♦ Allow for flexible appointments of officers to meet particular mission objectives.
- ♦ Rotate officers when appropriate between headquarters and corps/centres.

10. Personal and vocational growth in a changing and complex world

In the Army of the 21st century, initiative in mission comes from leaders who initiate their own personal and vocational development. Strong spiritual leaders undergo self-evaluation and develop a personal and vocational growth plan. They draw upon available resources to bring greater maturity to their personal and spiritual lives and greater competence to their leadership. They do this continually; they are always growing. This progress from strength to strength in their own development gives them confidence to be strong missional leaders.

A world of ever-new stimuli and endless distraction may tempt us to lose the focus of our calling. A society of ever-increasing complexity and change may diversify demands for service and stretch our ministry capacities. We can easily fall into mediocrity as we attempt to do far more than we can realistically achieve with real compassion and competence, and within the limitations of our human resources.

It will be the task of Army leaders to discover, amid the many things that 'could' be done in mission, what is 'worth' doing. Without this discrimination and decisiveness, the Army will attempt to do too many things, and do none of them well. It will fall inevitably into mediocrity.

How can the Army keep its focus on the important things? The answer lies in spiritual leaders who show the way, those whose lives are focused on calling, those who are 'moving on to perfection' both in their spiritual and in their vocational journey through life. These are officers, local officers and other leaders who invest in their own growth, improve their readiness for their particular callings and commit themselves to a personal development plan. Without this, their leadership will lose focus and be diminished.

The focused leaders needed for the 21st century will also have good mentors. Mentors will help leaders gain clarity about their calling and their temptations to ignore it. They will also help leaders to assess themselves and set worthwhile goals for spiritual, personal and vocational development. They will hold leaders accountable.

With the advantage of good mentors and growth plans, Army leaders will focus on what is important and teach other Salvationists to do the same. As leaders, they will model intentional growth for other believers. In the years ahead, a vital Army will encourage the personal and vocational growth of its leaders. It will continue to do so in the following key ways:

- Develop and implement a process for officers' self-evaluation and strategic growth.
- Train officers to take the lead in their own evaluation and goal setting.
- Train supervising officers to be consultants and coaches in this process.
- Encourage a reciprocal evaluation process.

Who is sufficient?

Who is sufficient for these things? How is such spiritual leadership possible? The sufficiency, of course, is of God alone (2 Corinthians 3:4-6).

Into our hands God has placed his liberating Word of life, a Word to preach and teach, and a Word through which to bring people to an encounter with God. The leader can receive as well as give as he or she uncovers the living presence of Christ in the world and invites the whosoever to experience the compassion of God and of Christ's Body, the Church.

In the Army, when we have been at our best, when we have been most effective in realising our calling, our spiritual leaders have been good preachers and doers of the Word. They have lived and led by the Word of Christ, and they have served by the reality of his presence. Perhaps, like Elisha, we can now pray that the mantle of our leaders gone before will continue to fall on us, so that we will also be able to lead people to places where God speaks and life is transformed.

For group discussion

1. Ask each group member to come prepared to identify the crucial challenges to spiritual leadership in his or her own vocational (work) setting and what is needed to meet those challenges.

2. Discuss the crucial challenges to spiritual leadership in your own corps setting.

3. Discuss the future of spiritual leadership in The Salvation Army:
   a. the greatest opportunities
   b. the greatest threats
   c. the most effective ways to develop and nurture the kind of spiritual leadership which you think our mission will require in the future.

CONCLUSION

A RECOMMENDATION from the 1995 International Conference of Salvation Army Leaders forms the background to the original 2002 publishing of this book, as General John Gowans indicated in the foreword. It requested, 'That the roles of officers and soldiers be defined and a biblical theology of priesthood be developed to encourage greater involvement in ministry (for example, spiritual leadership, leadership (in general), worship, service and evangelisation).' In response to that request, the 2002 edition sought to make those definitions and to develop that theology. The key point in that recommendation is, however, how all Salvationists are to be encouraged towards greater involvement in mission and ministry.

The book as a whole is an attempt to deal with that point. Salvationists should find encouragement towards greater involvement in ministry as they:

- ◆ Recognise that they are called by God to offer themselves in worship to him as members of the incarnational community of Jesus Christ, thereby fulfilling the Army's mission of preaching the gospel and meeting human needs in his name without discrimination.
- ◆ Have a renewed focus on their divine vocation as a royal priesthood gifted by the Holy Spirit for works of service so that the Body of Christ may be built up.
- ◆ See that, whether officers or soldiers, they are sent out by God for ministry in his world and in his Church, to be servants of their Servant Lord.
- ◆ Find themselves on a lifelong pilgrimage of being equipped more adequately to meet the need of the present age for

priests and prophets and true leaders who declare the praises of him who called them out of darkness into his wonderful light.

The Salvation Army's International Spiritual Life Commission Report of 1998 has a section entitled 'The disciplines of life in the Spirit'. That part of the report forms an appropriate conclusion to *Servants Together* – the whole people of God partnered in ministry. A renewal of our commitment to these disciplines will equip and enable us to become servants together with our Lord.

THE DISCIPLINES

The Disciplines of the Inner Life

We affirm that the consistent cultivation of the inner life is essential for our faith life and for our fighting fitness. The disciplines of the inner life include solitude, prayer and meditation, study and self-denial. Practising solitude, spending time alone with God, we discover the importance of silence, learn to listen to God and discover our true selves. Praying, we engage in a unique dialogue that encompasses adoration and confession, petition and intercession. As we meditate, we attend to God's transforming Word. As we study, we train our minds towards Christlikeness, allowing the Word of God to shape our thinking. Practising self-denial, we focus on God and grow in spiritual perception. We expose how our appetites can control us, and draw closer in experience, empathy and action to those who live with deprivation and scarcity.

The Disciplines of our Life Together

We affirm the unique fellowship of Salvationists worldwide. Our unity in the Holy Spirit is characterised by our shared vision, mission and joyful service. In our life together we share responsibility for one another's spiritual well-being. The vitality of our spiritual life is also enhanced by our accountability to one another, and when we practise the discipline of accountability our spiritual vision becomes objective, our decisions more balanced, and we gain the wisdom of the fellowship and the means to clarify and test our own thinking. Such spiritual direction may be provided effectively through a group or by an individual. Mutual accountability also provides the opportunity to confess failure or sin and receive the assurance of forgiveness and hope in Christ.

The Disciplines of our Life in the World

We affirm that commitment to Christ requires the offering of our lives in simplicity, submission and service. Practising simplicity we become people whose witness to the world is expressed by the values we live by, as well as by the message we proclaim. This leads to service which is a self-giving for the salvation and healing of a hurting world, as well as a prophetic witness in the face of social injustice.